*The publishers wish to thank Clive A. Lawton, the Reverend
Stephen Motyer and Martin Redfern for their kind help in the
preparation of this book.*

First published in the United Kingdom in 1983 by Kingfisher Books Limited,
Elsley Court, 20-22 Great Titchfield Street
London W1P 7AD

First United States publication in 1983 by Franklin Watts, Inc.,
387 Park Avenue South, New York, New York 10016

ISBN: 0-531-03592-1

Edited by Adrian Sington
Cover design by Pinpoint
Colour separations by Newsele Litho Ltd. Milan, Italy
Phototypeset by Southern Positives and Negatives (SPAN),
Lingfield, Surrey
Printed in Hong Kong by South China Printing Co.

Children's BIBLE

RETOLD BY JAMES BENTLEY

Illustrated by Colin and Moira Maclean

Franklin Watts **New York** **Toronto**

1983

Contents

THE OLD TESTAMENT

THE NEW TESTAMENT

THE OLD TESTAMENT

God Makes Everything

At first, everywhere was dark and empty. So God decided to make light. He made the stars that twinkle, and the sun, and the moon that shines at night. He made day and night, the sea and the land.

God decided to make a man to live in the world. But the man was all alone, so God created all the animals that roam the world – from the biggest to the tiniest. Then he made all the fish in the sea and all the birds in the heavens. The first man gave names to all these creatures, and God put him in charge of them all.

Even though the man had all the animals of the world, he was lonely. He wanted someone to live with and talk to. So God made him fall into a deep sleep. Then he took one of the man's ribs and used that to make the first woman. When the man woke, he saw the woman and said, "You are made of bone from my bones and flesh from my flesh."

God made them the most beautiful garden to live in. A river with four streams watered this garden. The place was called Eden. God said to the man and the woman, "Here you can have many children. And I have made for you plants and trees, which will give fruit, so that you need never be hungry."

The man and the woman had no clothes; but they didn't bother about this; it wasn't important. God said, "I want to make sure that you do what I tell you: there is one rule that you must obey. You can eat everything that grows in the garden, except the fruit of one tree. It is the tree which tells of what is good and evil."

They both listened carefully, and were very happy with what God had given them.

Genesis 1; Genesis 2.

Adam and Eve in the Garden of Eden

Of all the animals God had made, the most cunning was the serpent. One day the serpent asked the woman (who was called Eve), "Did God really say you mustn't eat the fruit from the trees in the garden?"

"No," replied Eve. "We can eat the fruit from the trees except the one in the middle. God said we mustn't eat that fruit if we don't want to die."

The serpent decided to try to make Eve disobey God. "You won't die, you know," he said. "You see, God doesn't want you to eat that fruit because if you do, you'll be as great as he is. He alone wants to say what is good and what is bad. If you eat of the fruit of the tree of good and evil, you will know as much as he does."

Eve looked at the tree. Its fruit looked delicious. She stretched out her hand and plucked some. She ate the fruit – and gave some to Adam.

A strange thing happened then. They looked at each other and said, "We've no clothes on." They were suddenly ashamed of themselves. They took the leaves of a nearby fig tree, sewed them together and covered themselves.

That evening, as it grew cooler, God came to walk in the Garden of Eden. Adam and Eve knew that they had done wrong and they hid in the trees. But God called, "Where are you?"

Adam replied, "I was frightened, because I was naked, and so I hid myself."

"Who told you that you were naked?" asked God. "You must have eaten the fruit of that tree in the middle of the garden." Then Adam tried to blame Eve, and Eve tried to blame the serpent for making them disobey God. But it was really their own fault. God was very angry. He said to the serpent, "Now I am going to make you crawl on your stomach in the dust. You and this woman and all her children will be enemies. They will stamp on your head and you will bite them."

God said to Eve, "You'll never be as happy again as you were in the Garden of Eden." And to Adam he said, "Now you will have to work and work and work to get enough food to live. You won't be working in the fine soil of the garden of Eden any longer. From now on before you can grow food you'll have to dig up thorns and thistles."

Then he looked at them and said, "One day you will both die."

So he drove Adam and Eve out of the garden. And at the entrance to it he put one of his heavenly servants, with a flaming sword to stop anyone else from coming in.

Genesis 3.

Cain Kills his Brother

The first two children of Adam and Eve were boys. The elder brother, Cain, was a farmer who grew the crops. The second son, Abel, was a shepherd.

Abel's sheep were very fine. Sometimes he would offer one or two of them to God. But the crops of Cain were terrible, and when he offered them to God, God was not pleased with them. Cain used to get angry and upset, but God warned him not to become bitter.

But still Cain had dreadful moods. One day, he said to his brother. "Let's go out." When they were alone in the countryside, they quarreled, and Cain killed his brother Abel.

God asked Cain, "Where is your brother Abel?" Cain replied, "I don't know. Is it my job to look after him?" God said, "I can hear your brother's blood crying to me from the

ground." And he drove Cain away from his family and from his land. "From now on." said God, "you'll be a wanderer over all the earth."

Cain said, "This is more than I can bear, I will be hidden from you. I have no one to protect me now. Anyone who wants to, can kill me."

God didn't want Cain to be killed, so he put a special mark on him. This mark protected him from those who wanted to kill him. Anyone who saw the mark would know that it was dangerous to strike Cain down.

Genesis 4, 1–16.

The Flood

Noah was a good man. But the men and women who lived at the time of Noah led wicked lives. God felt sorry that he had created them so he decided to destroy them. The only people that he would spare were Noah and his family.

God told Noah how to build a huge ship, called an ark. The ship was to have three decks big enough not only to take Noah and his family but at least two of every animal.

Noah did as God said. And God shut the door of the ark. Then God made it rain. It rained forty days and forty nights and flooded the land. When the rain stopped, the water was higher than the mountains. Everyone had been drowned.

Slowly, the waters ebbed and drained away. And in time the ark came to rest on a mountain called Ararat. Noah wondered whether it was safe to leave the ark. He opened a

porthole and released a raven. It flew around waiting for the water to disappear. Next, Noah let out a dove. The first time it could find no trees to perch on, so it returned. Seven days later, Noah let it out again. This time it flew back with a fresh olive twig in its beak. Noah now knew that the land was dry. He waited another seven days, and then let the dove out for a third time. This time it did not come back.

Noah said to everyone, "Come on out." Animals and people eagerly left the ark. God blessed Noah and his family. He told them to take care of each other and not to fight and kill. He also said that this was the first and last time he was going to flood the whole earth. At that moment, Noah looked up and saw, stretched across the sky, a beautiful rainbow. God said, "Every time you see a rainbow, you will remember my agreement."

Genesis 6, 5–22; Genesis 7; Genesis 8.

The Tower of Babel

At one time all the people of the earth spoke the same language. The people moved eastward until they came to a flat land in the country of Shinar. There they decided to settle and build their houses.

They learned how to make strong bricks by baking them for a long time in a fire. They boiled tar, until it became very thick and sticky. They used this to bond the bricks. They were pleased because they could now build bigger and bigger houses.

Some of them got together and decided to make a name for themselves. They wanted everyone to admire them. Now that they could build stronger and bigger houses they decided to build a whole town, and in it a great tower that would go higher and higher until its top reached into heaven.

Now God saw what was happening and thought how fool-

ish they were to think themselves so clever. He must do something to stop them or there would be no telling what they might do next. He decided to confuse their languages so that they could no longer understand one another. In this way the people were scattered all over the earth.

So they gave up building the town and the great tower. And they said, "This place 'Babel' must mean 'mixed up', because God has mixed up the way we all speak to each other."

Genesis 11, 1–9.

Abraham and Lot

In the land of Haran there lived a man called Abraham, a descendant of Noah. One day God said to him, "Leave Haran and go to a land which I will show you. I will make you and your children and their children into a great nation."

Abraham set off. With him went his wife Sarah, his many belongings and cattle, and his servants who looked after the cattle. He took also his nephew Lot, Lot's family and servants, and Lot's cattle. When they came to the land of Canaan, there wasn't enough room for them all to live together. So Abraham said to Lot, "You choose where you want to live, and I'll live in the land that is left."

Lot chose the plain of Jordan and went to live near the city of Sodom. In Sodom everyone lived evil lives. Once, for instance, Lot was giving shelter to two messengers from

God. The men of Sodom didn't like messengers from God. They came to Lot's house and said, "Send them out to us." They wanted to treat them cruelly. Lot wouldn't send out God's messengers. Some men of Sodom tried to smash down Lot's door to get into the house, but God's messengers struck them blind, so all they could do was grope around.

God decided to destroy the city of Sodom, because all its people were so wicked. Abraham said to God, "I think there may be fifty good men in Sodom. If you think so as well, please save the city." But God looked and couldn't find even ten good men, let alone fifty. He sent a messenger to tell Lot to leave. "Don't look back on the burning city," said the messenger. "Just leave as fast as you can." But Lot's wife couldn't resist. She was too inquisitive so she turned around to look at the burning city. As soon as she did that, she was turned into a pillar of salt, for disobeying God's message.

Genesis 12 to 19.

Abraham and Isaac

When Abraham and Sarah were very old they had a son. They called him Isaac. They had thought that they wouldn't have any children, because they were so old; but now they were very happy. They loved their son so much, that when he was a little older, Abraham gave a great party.

Isaac grew into a strong boy. Abraham loved him dearly. God now decided to test Abraham, to see if he would do anything God asked. He said to Abraham, "Take Isaac up into a mountain, that I shall point out to you, and there offer him to me. The only way you can do that is to kill him and then burn his body."

Heartbroken, Abraham chopped wood and loaded it on a donkey. Then, with two servants, he and Isaac set off. After three days, they saw the mountain. Abraham told the servants to stay with the donkey. He told them that he and Isaac were going to worship God in the mountain. They would kill and burn a lamb, or some other animal, and offer it to God. Then they would come back.

Abraham told Isaac to carry the wood. On the way up the mountain, Isaac grew puzzled. "We have the wood," he said to his father. "We can set it on fire. But where is the lamb we are going to burn on it?" Abraham replied, "Don't worry. God will give us something to burn." He couldn't bear to tell Isaac that he intended to kill him. Poor Abraham loved Isaac so much, but he still thought he should obey God's commands, even though they were so dreadful.

When they had climbed the mountain, Abraham built an altar and put wood on it. Then he tied up his son and laid him on the altar. He was just about to pick up the knife to kill his son when a loud voice called to him. "Abraham, Abraham, do not harm the boy. Now God knows you are his true servant. You were even prepared to kill your only son when God asked you to."

Abraham was overjoyed. Then looking round he saw a ram was trapped by its horns in a bush. So Abraham killed the ram instead of Isaac, and offered it to God.

God was pleased with Abraham. He never really intended to have Isaac killed, but Abraham hadn't known that. Now he said, "Because you would have given me your son – your only son – I will give you many many blessings. The people that come after you – your children, their children, and their children's children – will be more than the stars in the sky and the sands on the seashore. Their enemies will never defeat them. And every nation on earth will be glad that you lived."

So Abraham and Isaac went back to the servants. They all set off for a place called Beersheba, where Abraham made his home.

Genesis 21, 1–9; *Genesis 22*, 1–19.

Isaac and Rebecca

When Abraham was extremely old, he began to think about a wife for his son Isaac. He decided to send his most trusted servant back to their homeland to find Isaac a wife. Abraham insisted that Isaac should not marry a Canaanite girl because the Canaanites did not believe in God. Abraham didn't want Isaac to leave Canaan for God had promised that they should be blessed in their new land.

The servant set out with a caravan of Abraham's camels laden with precious things. He traveled to the land of Mesopotamia where Abraham had once lived.

He reached a city where Abraham's brother Nahor lived. Outside the city was a well. The servant thought of a plan to find a good wife for Isaac. He made his camels kneel down by the well. When the young women came out of the city to fetch their water, he would ask one of them for a drink. If she was

kind enough to offer some water to the camels as well, then he would know that she was the person to marry Isaac.

While he was still thinking of his plan, a girl called Rebecca came to the well. Her grandfather was Nahor, Abraham's brother. She lowered her water jar and filled it. The servant ran up to her and asked, "Please let me have a little water from your water jar." She gave him a drink, and then she said, "I'll now get some water for your camels to drink."

The servant knew that he had found the right girl and was pleased. He took a gold ring and two golden bracelets from Abraham's treasure. The gold ring was for the girl's nostril and the bracelets were for her arms.

When the servant asked Rebecca to tell him about herself, he also asked if he and his camels could stay the night in her brother's house. And she ran home to tell her brother all that had happened.

As soon as her brother, Laban, saw the ring and the bracelets, he knew that the man had something important to ask. Laban went to the well himself and helped Abraham's servant to bring the camels to his house.

At supper the servant refused to eat anything, until he had given them his important message – because he still did not know whether Rebecca would agree to be Isaac's wife. But when everyone heard the whole story, they said that God must have made it happen in that way. They asked Rebecca, "Do you want to leave with this man?" And she said, "Yes."

Laban and Rebecca's mother wanted her to stay with them a little longer, but she wanted to leave right away.

As they reached Abraham's home, they saw Isaac walking in the fields. Rebecca quickly put a veil over her face, to show that from now on she would belong only to Isaac. The servant told Isaac the story and when Isaac saw Rebecca, he was happy and glad she was to be his wife.

Genesis 24.

Jacob Tricks Esau

Isaac became very old and blind. It was time, he thought, to choose a new leader who would take his place when he died. He chose Esau, the elder of his twin sons.

Isaac decided to have a special meal and eat all his favorite food. He would then bless Esau, and everyone would know that he was to be the next leader.

Rebecca was very angry. She liked Jacob better than Esau and thought that Jacob would be a much better leader. Jacob had wanted to be leader too. One day, when Esau was very hungry, Jacob had said to him, "If I give you food will you let me become leader when our father dies?" Esau agreed to this.

Rebecca now thought of a plan to trick her old husband. While Esau was away, she would cook Isaac's favorite meal. Jacob would take the food to his father, pretending to be Esau, and Isaac would bless him by mistake and so make him leader. Jacob was frightened, because although Isaac was

blind he could still recognize people by touching them. He would know he was touching Jacob, because Jacob's arms were smooth and Esau's were hairy. If Isaac discovered that they were trying to trick him, he'd be angry. But Rebecca had thought of this and had covered Jacob's arms with hairy skins.

Poor Isaac was tricked. He wondered whether the voice he could hear was Jacob's or Esau's. But when he felt the hairy skins, he blessed Jacob, thinking that he was Esau, and said: "You shall rule over all your brothers. They must obey you." Isaac then prayed that God would make many other people serve Jacob too.

When Esau returned and learned what had happened, he wept with anger. "As soon as my father is dead," he said, "I will kill Jacob."

So Jacob ran away to escape from his brother. He married, became rich and had twelve sons.

Genesis 25, 29–34; Genesis 27; Genesis 29, 25–43.

Jacob Wrestles with God

Jacob wanted to make friends with his brother Esau, but he was still frightened of him. He was scared of the four hundred fighting men who went about with Esau. So Jacob tried to please his brother by sending many many presents. He sent 220 goats, 200 ewes and 10 rams, 30 mother camels, each with a baby camel, 40 cows, 10 bulls and 30 asses.

He also thought it might be safer to let his family meet Esau first, and join them later. Jacob had two wives (many men had two wives in those days), as well as two slave-girls and eleven children. They all waded across the river Jabbok, and went on ahead to meet Esau. Jacob stayed behind.

That night, a strange thing happened. Out of nowhere a

man appeared and began to wrestle with Jacob. They wrestled all night. The man was far stronger than Jacob; but Jacob fought and fought and wouldn't give in.

At last the man twisted Jacob's hip completely out of its socket. It was now daybreak, and the strange man wanted to leave; but Jacob clung on, though his hip must have hurt.

"Before I let go," he cried, "you must give me something." Jacob may not have won, but he didn't want to think that he had wrestled all night for nothing.

"All right," replied the man. And then he gave a clue to Jacob about who he was. "From now on," he said, "you'll be called Israel. That's because Israel means 'strong', and all night you've been strong fighting against God. You are not a weakling any more. Now you can be strong against men."

Jacob began to understand why the fight had been so hard. He'd been fighting God himself – God disguised as a man.

He was amazed. Most people see God only when they've died. He'd seen God face to face, and he was still alive. "I can't wait to tell people about this." he thought. "I'll call the place where God and I wrestled Peniel, because that means 'face of God.' Whenever people come here, they'll remember what happened."

And people *did* remember. Even today, to remind themselves of what God did at Peniel to Jacob's hip, Jews will not eat flesh taken from an animal's hip.

Jacob was pleased, even though he was in pain. He hoped God would make his children strong too; and their children.

And he thought, "I don't want to fight against God anymore. In the past, I was always fighting him, going against what he wanted in all sorts of ways. Last night he showed me that if you fight against God, you can't win."

So Jacob went limping after his family, ready to make things up with Esau.

Genesis 32, 13–32.

Joseph

Jacob, now called Israel, was a wanderer. He never stayed long in one place. People called his children and their children and all that came after them the "children of Israel".

Israel was an old man when his youngest son Joseph was born. He spoiled the little boy. Joseph seemed to get the most of everything; much more than his brothers. His father made him a beautiful coat with long sleeves. When his brothers saw it, they were angry. Their father had never given them anything like that.

Joseph's Brothers Sell Him

Joseph was spoiled by his father. He once dreamed that his brothers bowed down to him. Once his dream was so strange that he felt he must tell his brothers about it. Joseph said that in the dream they were all putting long stalks of wheat into sheaves and standing them up in the fields. Suddenly all his brothers' sheaves bowed down to Joseph's sheaf.

Joseph was very silly to tell this dream to his brothers. They said, "So you want to rule us, do you?" This made Joseph's brothers very angry indeed. Even Joseph's father was annoyed. "Do you expect me and your mother to bow down as well?" he asked.

Joseph's brothers now hated him so much that they decided to get rid of him. One day, they were a long way from home looking after some animals. Israel asked Joseph to go and see if his brothers were all right. When his brothers saw him coming, they decided that they would kill him and throw him into a deep hole, and tell Israel that a wild animal had killed him.

But the oldest son, Reuben, did not want to kill Joseph. He worked out a plan to save him. He told the brothers to put Joseph down a deep, empty well. (Reuben's plan was to come back later and pull Joseph out.) The brothers thought this a better idea. They took off Joseph's coat and threw him down the well.

They were just starting a meal, when some traders went by, riding on camels. The traders were on their way to Egypt. One brother called Judah had another idea. He told his brothers to sell Joseph as a slave to these merchants.

So they pulled Joseph out of the well and the traders bought him for twenty pieces of silver. The brothers kept Joseph's coat and dipped it in goat's blood. They took it back to their father, pretending that they had found it somewhere. Israel looked at the coat and said, "It's my son's. A wild animal must have killed him." He was so sad, he wept.

What about poor Joseph? When the traders reached Egypt, they sold him again to a man named Potiphar, who was an important friend of the ruler of Egypt called the Pharaoh.

Genesis 37.

Joseph's Adventures in Egypt

Joseph's new master Potiphar soon saw how well he worked, so he put him in charge of his whole household. But Potiphar's wife used to flirt with Joseph. Joseph didn't like this, because he didn't want to steal someone else's wife, and also he liked Potiphar. But the woman grew very angry. She lied to Potiphar about Joseph. She stole Joseph's coat, and then told Potiphar that Joseph had left it in her room when he came to insult her. Potiphar believed his wife and put Joseph in prison.

Even in prison, Joseph's honest ways helped him. He was soon put in charge of other prisoners. And there he met two men who had been imprisoned by Pharaoh himself. One of them had looked after Pharaoh's wine; the other had baked his bread. One day they both had strange dreams. Joseph knew a lot about dreams, so they told him about them.

The wine-keeper dreamed of a vine which had three branches. In the dream he took grapes from the vine and then squeezed a drink from them into Pharaoh's cup. Joseph said that meant that in three days' time he would be taken back into Pharaoh's service.

The baker dreamed of carrying three trays of Pharaoh's favorite cakes on top of his head. Unfortunately, the birds came and ate the cakes. Joseph said that was sad. It meant that in three days' time the baker would be put to death by an angry Pharaoh.

Everything happened just as Joseph said it would. When the keeper of the Pharaoh's wine was leaving prison, Joseph asked him to say some good things about him to Pharaoh; but the man forgot all about Joseph until much later, when Pharaoh himself had two very strange dreams.

First, Pharaoh dreamed that he was standing on a bank of the river Nile. He saw seven fat cattle coming up from the river and eating the rich grass; but then seven very thin cattle came and ate the fat cattle.

Genesis 39.

The Pharaoh Sends for Joseph

Pharaoh's next dream was about wheat growing in the fields. On one wheat stalk he saw seven ears of wheat, full and ripe; but after that, in his dream, came seven miserably thin ears, which swallowed up the ripe fat ones.

Pharaoh didn't know what these dreams meant, and they puzzled him. He told his magicians about the dreams, but not one of them could understand their meaning. But then his wine-keeper suddenly remembered Joseph and told Pharaoh to ask his help. Joseph knew what all the dreams meant. He told Pharaoh that for seven years there would be lots of good food grown in Egypt. The cattle would grow fat. But for seven years after that, hardly any food would grow. It was important to save and save as much as possible during the seven good years.

Pharaoh was very grateful and made Joseph chief ruler in all Egypt. He gave Joseph a beautiful gold ring, fine clothes

and a splendid chariot to ride in. Joseph took an Egyptian name and an Egyptian wife. He was now thirty years old.

Everything happened as he had told Pharaoh. During the seven good years Joseph went everywhere in Egypt, taking the wheat from the countryside and storing it in the towns. Soon nobody could count how much wheat he had stored. But when the bad years came, people began to starve. Then they came to Pharaoh, and said, "Give us bread." But Pharaoh said, "Go to see Joseph."

Joseph now sold wheat to the Egyptians. And soon people from other countries came to buy wheat from him, because during the seven bad years no food grew anywhere.

So although sometimes things seemed to be going badly for Joseph, God was always with him. Sometimes he was lucky, sometimes unhappy, but always he knew that God would make everything come out right for him.

Genesis 40; Genesis 41.

Joseph Meets his Brothers Again

No food grew anywhere during the seven bad years, and Joseph's brothers and his old father had nothing to eat. Israel decided to send them to buy wheat in Egypt. So they came to Joseph.

As soon as he saw them, Joseph recognized them all. But he had only been a boy when they sold him, and after so long they no longer recognized him. He decided to test them, to see if they had changed since he lived with them.

First of all he said they were spies who had come to find out how another country could beat Egypt in battle. They became angry and Joseph put them in prison for three days.

Then he asked them questions about their father. They told him that the old man had never stopped missing Joseph, but now Israel loved, above all, little Benjamin and had kept him at home. Joseph then said he would believe they weren't spies if they would bring Benjamin to Egypt to see him. He let them return home to fetch Benjamin, but he made them leave Simeon behind.

The brothers thought all this must be a punishment from God for what they had done to Joseph long ago. When they arrived home with the sacks of wheat which they had bought they found that the money they had used to pay for it had been put into the sacks. They were troubled and wondered what to do.

Israel didn't want Benjamin to go to Egypt; he loved him so much. But soon their food ran out again, and he had no choice. So the brothers, this time with Benjamin, went to Egypt a second time. And when they arrived Joseph prepared a great banquet for them. He gave Benjamin five times as much food as anyone else.

During the banquet, unknown to Benjamin, Joseph arranged for his own special silver cup to be put in the sack of wheat that Benjamin was to take home with him. The next day, the brothers were sent off with their donkeys. They had not gone far when Joseph said to his chief servant, "Follow them and when you catch up with them ask why they have repaid my kindness by stealing from me." When he caught up with them, the chief servant found the silver cup in Benjamin's sack and accused him of stealing it. They went back to Joseph who said he would keep Benjamin as a slave.

The brothers were horrified. One brother, Judah, begged Joseph to change his mind. "If I went back to my father without little Benjamin," he said, "it would break my father's heart. Please let me be your slave instead."

Joseph couldn't pretend anymore and told them who he was. They hurried home to tell their father the good news that Joseph was alive and a great man. They all returned to Egypt and had all they needed for the rest of their lives.

Genesis 42 to Genesis 50.

Moses: A Baby in the Bulrushes

After a long time, the Pharaohs of Egypt forgot all about Joseph. One of them began to be afraid that there were too many of the children of Israel in Egypt. "Maybe," he thought, "they will join with other kings and beat me in battle." So he made them into slaves and gave orders that every new-born son of an Israelite should be killed.

One Israelite woman was determined that this should not happen to her new baby boy. She hid him for three months inside her house. He was a fine strong son. But soon he would be too big to hide.

So she made a basket for him, covering it with tar to make it watertight. She put her son in it and hid it among the bulrushes at the edge of the river.

Soon the daughter of Pharaoh came down to the river to bathe. She saw the basket and sent one of her maids to fetch it. She knew he must be a son of the Israelites. But the baby was crying, and she felt sorry for him.

Now, one of the baby boy's elder sisters was watching all this. She ran up to Pharaoh's daughter and said, "Shall I go and find an Israelite woman to feed the baby for you?" Pharaoh's daughter agreed, and the girl ran to bring the baby's own mother.

So the baby was saved. His mother fed him and brought him up. When the boy grew older, his mother took him to Pharaoh's daughter, who treated him as if he were her own son.

She gave him the name: "Moses", which means "drawn out"; and to explain it, Pharaoh's daughter said, "I drew him out of the water."

Exodus 1; Exodus 2, 1–10.

Moses and the Evil Pharaoh

When Moses grew up, he soon knew he had to choose
between being on the side of the Egyptians and being on the
side of his own people. One day he saw an Egyptian hit one of
his own countrymen. This made Moses very angry. He killed
the Egyptian and buried him in the sand. But somebody told
Pharaoh what had happened, and he planned to kill Moses as
punishment. Moses had to leave quickly for a far-off country.

One day God attracted Moses' attention. Moses was on a
mountainside when he saw a bush on fire. The bush burned
and burned but it didn't burn to the ground. Then he heard
God's voice telling him that the children of Israel wouldn't
have to live any more under the rule of Pharaoh. Moses was to
lead them out of Egypt to freedom.

Moses grew frightened, because he didn't think he could
be a leader. But God gave him some powerful signs. One of
them was to turn Moses' stick into a snake and then turn it

back into a stick again. When Moses saw all this he felt happier and stronger. God said that Moses' brother Aaron should go with him to speak to Pharaoh because Moses was not a good speaker.

Moses and Aaron returned to Egypt. They went to Pharaoh to ask him to let the children of Israel go so that they could hold a feast in God's honor in the desert. But Pharaoh wouldn't let them.

Instead, Pharaoh said they must now work harder. If they didn't make enough bricks, he would have them flogged. And they must find their own materials to make the bricks. The children of Israel were furious with Moses and Aaron because they had upset Pharaoh who was now making their lives even more of a misery. So Moses and Aaron tried to frighten Pharaoh. They turned Aaron's stick into a snake. But Pharaoh's helpers turned *their* sticks into snakes. Aaron's snake gobbled up their snakes; but still Pharaoh refused to allow the children of Israel to leave.

God said that as they had tried everything to persuade Pharaoh to change his mind, there was nothing left but punishment. Altogether it took ten punishments – each one more terrible than the one that had gone before – before he finally let the Israelites go.

First, God with Moses' help, turned the river into blood, so that all the fishes died and nobody could drink the water. Then he punished the Egyptians by sending thousands and thousands of frogs into their bedrooms, on their beds, in the ovens and in the palace – everywhere. This time, Pharaoh said he would let the Israelites worship God in the desert; but when Moses removed the frogs, Pharaoh changed his mind.

Moses was angry and brought thousands of mosquitoes to bite and torment the Egyptians and their animals. Then he brought thousands and thousands of flies to pester them. These flies never went near the homes of the children of Israel. But still Pharaoh would not give in. He stuck it out even when Moses made all the Egyptian cattle – though not

the Israelite cattle – die of a deadly disease.

Again and again Pharaoh broke his word to Moses. Moses made all the Egyptians break out in boils. He made hailstones and fire ruin their crops and kill many of their people. He sent locusts to eat up everything growing in the fields. And then for three days there was darkness.

Sometimes Pharaoh would say that just a few Israelites – not all of them – could worship God. Sometimes he said they could go but had to leave their cattle behind. And sometimes he just changed his mind and said, "No." Finally he said to Moses, "Get out of my sight. If I see you again, I'll have you killed."

Pharaoh did not know that soon he himself would die. And he did not know that the tenth, most terrible punishment of all was still to come.

Exodus 3 to Exodus 10

The Passover

God now knew that there was no way of making Pharaoh let the children of Israel go without the greatest cruelty. So God told Moses to tell Pharaoh that the oldest child of every family and animal in the land of Egypt would die. And God would see that this did not happen to the children and animals of the Israelites.

Moses told the Israelites what to do. On the tenth day of the month, every man was to take either a sheep or a goat big enough to feed his family. If the family was too small to eat a whole animal, they were to join with neighbors and share theirs. On the fourteenth day of the month, all the Israelites would kill their animals together.

Moses said they were to smear some animal blood over the doorposts of every Israelite house. "When God goes through the land to kill every oldest child," said Moses, "he will see the blood on the doorposts and pass over your houses." In that way no Israelite would be killed.

Then Moses told them to be ready for a journey – with their shoes on their feet and their walking staffs in their hands. They were all to eat a meal. The meat from the sheep or goat was to be roasted over a fire. They were to eat it quickly, with some bitter herbs. All of it must be eaten – head, feet and entrails. They were not to wait for the bread to rise, but were to eat it as a kind of flat cake.

"In the years to come," Moses told them, "you must keep this day every year as a special day – a day of remembrance. Because God passed over your oldest children, you will call it the feast of the Passover. You must make sure your children never forget this."

They did everything he told them. And in the middle of the night every Egyptian family found the oldest child dead. Pharaoh's eldest son, the heir to the throne, was dead. Pharaoh called Moses and Aaron to him. "Go away, all of you," he said. "Worship your God in the desert. Take your cattle and all your people but please go. And ask your God to bless me, or else I and all my people will be dead."

The Journey Begins
The children of Israel were all ready. They had their clothes in bundles on their backs. Although they had strong men who could fight anyone who attacked them, God knew they would be disturbed if they came upon a fierce people called the Philistines, who lived in the desert. So he led them by a roundabout route, so as to miss the Philistines.

It was a long journey. So that they wouldn't lose their way, God led them during the day by a pillar of cloud which went in front of them. At night they couldn't see the cloud, so God lit their way with a pillar of fire. He wanted them to march day and night so they would get as far away from Pharaoh as possible.

And Moses took with him the bones of Joseph, who so long ago had first brought the children of Israel to Egypt.

Exodus 11; Exodus 12; Exodus 13.

The Exodus

Now Pharaoh was extremely angry with himself for letting the Israelites go. And his people said, "Why did you allow them to stop working for us?" So he pursued them with an army, with men on horses and with chariots.

The children of Israel were frightened again. Once more they blamed Moses for what was happening, "We might as well have died in Egypt, as die here in the desert."

But Moses trusted in God. By day God concealed the Israelites from the Egyptians by putting the pillar of cloud behind the Israelites. At night God led them with the pillar of fire.

Even so, the Egyptians were catching up with the Israelites by the time they came to the Red Sea. Moses pointed across the sea. That was the way the Israelites had to go. But how could they cross it? Suddenly, a great wind rose up. It blew from the east all night. In the morning the Israelites saw that it had blown back part of the sea and there was dry land for them to walk on. And over they all went, with the waters piled up on either side.

The Egyptians were by now close behind them. The horsemen and the army and the chariots chased after them where the sea had been blown back. Of course, the ground was still muddy, and so some of the chariot wheels stuck and the drivers and horses couldn't budge them.

Moses again stretched out his hand over the sea, and the water began to flow back. The Egyptian army was still trying to free the chariots from the mud. As the waters returned they flowed over the whole army. The soldiers struggled to escape, but every single one was drowned. At last God had let the Israelites go free.

Everyone was so happy that they all began to sing a song in praise of God:

"God is wonderful:
He has thrown the horse and rider into the sea,
God has saved me.
The chariots and Pharaoh's army are drowned in the
Red Sea.
God will rule us for ever."

Exodus 14, 15.

47

The Manna and the Quails

The Israelites continued their journey across the desert. Sometimes there was no water to drink, but in the end Moses always seemed to find somewhere pleasant to stay. Once they stayed at a place called Elim, which had twelve water springs and seventy palm trees.

The Israelites Complain

As they reached the desert of Sinai, all the Israelites began to complain to Moses and Aaron, "Why did we not stay in Egypt where, at least, we were able to sit down to pans of meat and could eat bread to our heart's content? As it is, you have brought us to this wilderness so that we shall starve to death."

Then God said to Moses, "I will feed you all." And as he fed them he taught them a lesson: to trust in him and not to be so greedy.

And so it happened. In the evening quails flew over the camp and the Israelites caught them. In the morning, there was a coating of dew on the ground. When the dew lifted, the Israelites found delicate white food on the ground. God told them to gather just enough for each person's family for one day, and no more. If anyone gathered more than they could eat in one day and saved it for the next, it would go bad.

The children of Israel said when they saw the food, "What is it?", which in their language is "manna?". This explains how this food got its name. Manna looked like little seeds but tasted like beautiful honey wafers.

Exodus 16.

The Ten Commandments

As the children of Israel reached Mount Sinai, God called down to Moses to find out if the Israelites really wanted to obey him. They all said, "Yes," and Moses went up the mountain to meet God.

The people stayed at the foot of the mountain. Hearing the thunderclaps and seeing the smoke and fire on top of the mountain they were frightened. On two flat stones God gave his ten main rules or Commandments for all the people. These were:

1. You shall only have me for God. Do not let people try to make you worship the gods they bow down to.

2. Do not make gods out of melted metal. Do not try to carve a god and worship that.
3. Treat my name with respect.
4. Only work on the first six days of the week. Once you had to work all the time for the Egyptians, but I rescued you so that you could worship me. So on the seventh day of the week all of you – men, women, children, animals – must rest and you, who are my people, will worship me.
5. Love and honor your parents.
6. Do not murder people.
7. Do not take another person's wife or husband.
8. Do not steal anything.
9. Never say anything about your neighbor that isn't true.
10. Do not long for things that do not belong to you but belong to somebody else.

Moses gave many many other laws to the Israelites. He showed them how to worship God. Some Israelites took the name 'priests' and led the people in worship.

Moses told them that they could keep slaves, but only for six years, and then the slaves must go free. He told them what to do if somebody by accident killed another person's donkey or knocked out someone's tooth. Moses worked out, with the help of God, all sorts of other rules as well.

But none of them was so important as the Ten Commandments written on the flat stones which God gave to Moses. Even so, they were still amazing rules. Moses told the Israelites that God wanted them to be kind even to their enemies. If an Israelite saw that the donkey of a man who hated him had fallen because its load was too heavy, he had to go and try to help the man. If he saw his enemy's animals lost, he had to take them back to him.

Moses also never let the Israelites forget that they had to keep the feast of the Passover every year. As they would soon be able to start farming again, he said they had to thank God twice a year when they took in crops from the fields.

But for some of the Israelites, these rules were too difficult and more than they wanted to keep, even though God had been so good to them.

Exodus 19 to 24; Exodus 34, 10–28; Deuteronomy 5, 6–21.

The Golden Calf

Moses was a long time on Mount Sinai, talking with God. The children of Israel feared he might never come back. They felt that the God who had led them so far might abandon them now. So they asked Aaron to find them another god.

Aaron was a weak person. He told the people to give him all their golden earrings, with which he made a model of a calf. Then they all said, "This is the god who brought us out of Egypt." They bowed to it and danced around it.

God and Moses were very angry. God was so angry that he said he would destroy them all, leaving only Moses. But Moses thought about the promises God had made to Abraham, Isaac and Jacob. Some Israelites must be spared, if God was to keep those promises. So Moses said he would take revenge, but not on all the people.

Moses came down the mountain and saw the people dancing round the golden calf. He shouted in fury, "Who is on the side of the real God?" The sons of a man called Levi ran up to him. Moses ordered them to kill three thousand Israelites worshiping the golden calf.

In his rage, Moses smashed on the ground the two flat stones on which God had written the ten main rules. He flung the golden calf into the fire. When it had melted, he ground what was left into powder, mixed it with water, and made the children of Israel drink it. They never forgot his anger.

Moses went back to God. He took two more flat stones, and God wrote out again the ten main rules. Moses came down from the mountain. His face was shining so much that for a time he wore a veil when anyone spoke to him.

Moses made a huge box and in it he placed the two flat stones. The Israelites carried it wherever they went. They called it the "ark."

Exodus 32 to 34; Exodus 40.

The Death of Moses

For forty years Moses led the children of Israel through the desert. All the time he was planning to enter the land of Canaan, where long ago God had brought Abraham. Sometimes the people didn't do as he commanded. Sometimes they complained because they were hungry and thirsty. Sometimes other tribes attacked them. But always Moses managed to keep them safe, to find them water and food, and in the end to make them obey God's rules.

As they neared Canaan, Moses sent people ahead to see what the country was like. They spent forty days there, and they brought back beautiful grapes and pomegranates and figs. They said it was like a land which flowed with milk and honey. But they also said that the people who lived there were very dangerous. Some of them were extremely tall and strong.

When they heard this, some of the Israelites were so frightened that they wanted to go back to Egypt. They said

they would find a new leader who would do what they wanted. But two of Moses' chief helpers, Joshua and Caleb, said, "No. If God has brought us so far, and if God wants us to live in the land of Canaan, he will give it to us. We must go forward."

Moses was now very old. God had told him that he would not be leading his people across the river Jordan into the promised land, after all. They would get there; but they had to know that it was God – and no one else – who gave them everything.

Moses called Joshua and in front of everybody said, "Be strong. God will lead you into the promised land without me. He won't leave you. God will destroy the people who oppose you. Do not worry about anything at all."

Then Moses sang a long and marvelous song. In this song he blessed each of the twelve groups or tribes, the descendants of the twelve sons of Israel.

Before he died Moses had to see the promised land, even though he would die before the children of Israel reached it. He climbed the highest mountain, from which he could see Canaan, the land God was giving to the twelve tribes of Israel. Although he was very old, his eyes were still strong, and he saw the land for which he had struggled so long.

Then Moses came down into the plain, called Moab. There Moses died and was buried, though no one has ever been able to find his grave. One of his followers wrote, "Since then there has never been such a man in Israel as Moses, the man whom God knew face to face."

Numbers 13; Numbers 14, 1–9; Deuteronomy 31, 1–8; Deuteronomy 33 and 34.

Joshua Sends Spies into Canaan

Joshua was now leader of the children of Israel. He decided that they should not waste any more time before they entered the promised land. But he knew it would not be easy, as they would find many enemies there.

"We shall take over the city of Jericho," he said. "God has promised it to us." Joshua sent two spies to find out what their enemies in Canaan were thinking. They came to Jericho where they stayed at the house of a woman called Rahab.

Rahab's house was on the edge of the city wall. The King of Jericho thought the two spies might be there and sent soldiers to order Rahab to turn them out. The soldiers hurried to Rahab's house. Just before they arrived, Rahab hid the spies on the flat roof of her house under some rushes. When the soldiers came, she told them that she didn't know where the spies were. "They have been here," she lied, "but when the time came to shut the city gate, they left."

When the soldiers had gone, Rahab told the spies that everyone in Canaan was frightened of the Israelites. They had all heard what God had done for them – how he had drowned the Egyptians and beaten off tribes that had attacked them in the desert. She said, "No one is brave enough to stand up to you, because everyone knows that God is on your side."

The spies were happy to hear this news. Then Rahab let the spies down through the window by a rope. Because her house was on the city wall, they were now outside Jericho. They hid in the hills for three days, and then returned to Joshua to tell him the good news that their enemies were terrified of the children of Israel.

Joshua 2.

The Battle of Jericho

The King of Jericho was now frightened. He bolted the gates
of the city. Meanwhile, as Joshua thought of ways to capture
Jericho, God told him what to do.

He called the priests to him and told seven of them to take
trumpets made from rams' horns. They would lead the army.
A group of soldiers protected the priests. Then came the ark
which Moses had made (carried by more priests), followed
by the rest of the soldiers.

Joshua ordered them to march around Jericho, while the
priests blew their trumpets. Then they returned and spent
the night in their camp. The next day they marched around
the city again, blowing the trumpets as before.

They did this same thing for six days.

On the seventh day they rose at dawn and marched around

the city, blowing the trumpets as before. But this time they went around Jericho not once but seven times. Joshua said, "Wait till I give you the word. Then everyone must shout a war cry. We shall then capture the city and kill every living thing in it except Rahab and her relatives." The Israelites had made a promise to Rahab. If she didn't tell the King of Jericho anything when the Israelites attacked his city, she and all her family would be saved. All she had to do was to get all her relatives into her house and tie a red cord to the window, so that the Israelites would know which house was hers when they attacked the city.

Then Joshua gave the order. The soldiers shouted. The trumpets sounded. All the people cried out. The walls of Jericho came tumbling down. The children of Israel poured into the city, killing everything and everyone in their way. Only Rahab and her relatives were spared.

The Israelites took all the silver and gold of Jericho. They kept also the bronze and iron goods, putting it into the treasury of God. Then they burned the city to the ground.

This was Joshua's first victory. But he had not yet finished conquering Canaan. It took many many years. There was only one tribe (called the Hivites) that made peace with the Israelites without a fight, and that was through trickery. The Hivites dressed up in shabby clothes and sandals and pretended that they had walked miles to worship God. The Israelites promised not to harm their land, thinking it to be a long way away. But really they lived very close. When the Israelites discovered how they had been tricked they were angry. They could not break their promise by fighting them, so the Israelites condemned the Hivites to be their slaves. Altogether, Joshua had to fight thirty-one kings and their armies. And he was the one who finally divided the land among the tribes of the children of Israel.

Joshua 6; Joshua 9, 3–15; Joshua 12, 7–24.

Deborah and Barak

The children of Israel were now guided by judges. These were wise men and women who settled problems for the people. One of these judges was a woman called Deborah. She would sit under a palm tree, and if two people disagreed about something, they would come to see her and she would decide who was right.

Deborah also had other, more difficult things to do. The Israelites were often still attacked by other tribes, and she had to teach them how to defend themselves.

Once King Jabin of Hazor in northern Canaan decided to attack them. He had many troops and nine hundred chariots covered in iron. The commander of his army was called Sisera.

Deborah sent for a man called Barak. Sisera and his army were camped on Mount Tabor. Deborah told Barak, "Take ten thousand men and attack him." But Barak said, "I'll go

only if you come with me, for you speak on behalf of God and can tell us the right things to do." So Deborah went with him. Barak and his ten thousand men charged down Mount Tabor at the army of Sisera. When Sisera's soldiers saw them galloping down the hill, they ran away, with Barak's men following after them, hoping to kill them all.

Sisera ran away too. He saw a tent. It belonged to a woman called Jael. As she wasn't an Israelite, Sisera thought he might be safe inside her tent. "Don't tell anyone I'm here," he said, as he crept inside the tent.

But Jael was secretly on the side of the Israelites. She gave Sisera something to drink which made him fall fast asleep. Then she took a tent peg and drove it into his head.

When Deborah and Barak heard about it, they were happy, and sang a song because the commander of King Jabin's army was dead.

Judges 4 and 5.

Gideon

In the land of Canaan the other people living there worshiped all sorts of strange gods. Some Israelites started to do the same. For instance, many of them began to worship a god called Baal. They even built an altar of stone on which they could burn animals, as a way of worshiping him. Next to it they put up a great pole to show they thought Baal was great.

These Israelites had forgotten their promise to worship only God, who had brought them safely from Egypt. At this time the Israelites were being attacked by the Midianites and the Amalekites, who had joined together against them. Whenever an Israelite planted some corn, they would come and destroy it. Many Israelites had to live in the mountains to escape from these enemies.

God decided to get rid of Baal worship among his people, and also to free them from the Midianites and Amalekites. He called a man named Gideon, and told him to pull down the altar and the great pole of Baal, and to burn a calf to God.

Gideon was afraid to do this by day, but he did so by night.

When they found out about it, some Israelites wanted to kill Gideon; but they soon realized that the false god Baal didn't really exist. After all, his altar and pole had been smashed down and nothing evil had happened to anyone. Then Gideon said he wanted to free the Israelites from the cruelties of the Midianites and the Amalekites. Thirty-two thousand Israelites said they would fight with him.

God said that was too many. He didn't want the Israelites to think they had got rid of their cruel enemies with their own strength. He wanted them to see the power of God and know that he had done it for them. So Gideon said that any man who was afraid to fight should go home. Twenty-two thousand men left; but God said there were still too many.

He told Gideon to order the men to drink from a stream. Most of them knelt down and lapped up the water with their tongues. But three hundred of them raised the water to their mouths with their hands. God said, "We shall have just those three hundred."

All the enemy was in a camp on the plain of Jezreel. They stretched as far as the eye could see. Gideon sent two spies to their camp, and discovered that the enemy was afraid.

He divided his men into three groups. Each person had a trumpet, made of horn. As night fell, Gideon gave each man a large jar. Hidden inside each jar was a burning torch. At a signal from Gideon, they all blew their horns, smashed their jars to make a great noise, and waved their flaming torches. The Midianites and Amalekites were terrified. Some were so frightened and confused that they even killed each other in the darkness. All of them ran away.

For forty years while Gideon lived, the children of Israel lived in peace. But when he died, they all went back to their bad ways and started worshiping Baal again.

Judges 6 to 8.

Samson's Great Strength

The Israelites had stopped worshiping God, so he left them for a time to be ruled by another fierce tribe – the Philistines. Then God decided to free them. A boy called Samson was born. His parents never cut his hair. This was a sign that he belonged to God in a special way. Samson grew up to be a very strong man, so strong that once when a lion sprang at him, he tore it into pieces. Soon everyone heard about his amazing strength.

Samson fell in love with a Philistine girl. His parents didn't like this, because they wished him to marry an Israelite. But Samson wanted his own way. God allowed this to happen.

During Samson's wedding party, the Philistines were so frightened of his amazing strength that thirty men kept watch on him all the time. On his way to the wedding party, Samson had seen that bees had made their home in the body of the lion he had killed. While he was eating some of the honey, he thought of this riddle. "Tell me how a great greedy strong beast can give you the sweetest taste of your life." He asked his guests this riddle, but none of them knew the answer. Samson gave everyone seven days to answer it. If anyone could, Samson promised to give him thirty pieces of cloth and thirty sets of clothes.

Nobody could find the answer. But some of them persuaded Samson's wife to get the answer out of him and tell them. On the seventh day, they said to him, "We know the answer. Nothing is stronger than a lion; and nothing is sweeter than honey."

Samson became very angry. He knew that his wife must have told them the answer. He killed thirty Philistines, took their clothes, and gave them to those who had answered the riddle. Then Samson went home alone. Samson's wife then married a Philistine.

When Samson heard of this, he was enraged. He decided to

get even by wrecking the Philistines' wheat harvest. He took three hundred foxes and tied them in twos, tail to tail. To their tails he fastened torches, which he set fire to. Then he let them loose in the wheat. They burned up not only the wheat but also all the Philistines' vines and olive trees.

The Philistines assembled their army to kill Samson. They knew he was with some men in a place called Judah, so they planned to attack them there.

The men said, "Why are you attacking us? You want only Samson. We'll give him to you." Samson said he would let them tie him up and give him to the Philistines. So they tied Samson up and handed him to his enemies.

But Samson was too strong for them. He easily broke out of the ropes that tied him. He picked up the jawbone of a dead donkey and killed a thousand Philistines with it. Flinging it away, he sang at the top of his voice,

"I beat them with the jawbone of a donkey;
With the jawbone, I killed a thousand men."

Judges 14 and 15.

Samson and Delilah *Judges 16.*

The Philistines often tried to catch and kill Samson. One day, he fell in love with a woman called Delilah. The Philistine leaders came to her and said, "Ask Samson to tell you why he is so strong and we'll give you lots of silver."

At first Samson kept tricking her. He said, "If anyone ties me up with seven fresh branches of a willowtree, I'll be as weak as anyone else." When he fell asleep Delilah tied him up with willow sticks, and then shouted, "The Philistines have come to get you." But he broke free.

Next, he said that if he were tied up with new, unused ropes, he'd lose his strength. Again Delilah tied him up when he was asleep, but he broke free the moment she shouted.

The third time he said, "I'll be helpless if you weave seven locks of my hair into the cloth on your loom." She did so when next he was asleep, but this did not work either.

Delilah was now upset. "You've tricked me three times," she said. "You don't love me. Please tell me the truth about your strength." At last he told her. "I promised God I would never cut my hair. If my hair is cut off, I'll lose my strength." And so, when he slept, she got a man to shave off seven locks from his head. She cried, "The Philistines have come to get you." He awoke – but Samson's strength had gone.

They put a double chain around him. They put out his eyes and they made him turn a mill wheel in the city of Gaza.

The Philistines were happy. Their chiefs held a feast, and praised their god, Dagon. They were all sitting in Dagon's temple, which was huge, supported on pillars, when some of them said, "Get Samson out so that we can make fun of him."

But Samson's hair had begun to grow again. He prayed to God, "Give me my strength back, just once more." The blind Samson stood between the two main pillars and pushed. The stones and pillars came crashing down, killing Samson and all the Philistines in Dagon's temple.

The Story of Ruth

Some people thought that God looked after people only in the land of Canaan. This was not so, as the story of Ruth shows.

Ruth lived in a place called Moab. She was married to a man who came from Bethlehem. His mother was called Naomi, and she was a widow. After ten years, Ruth's husband died. And so did his brother. The brother's wife went back to her own family. So now Naomi was left alone in the world, save for Ruth.

She said to Ruth, "You should go back to your own family, as your sister-in-law has done." But Ruth said, "No. Wherever you go, I will go. Wherever you live, I will live. I will worship your God too." She wouldn't leave Naomi on her own.

The two women went back to Bethlehem, where Naomi had some land she could sell. They arrived there just at the

time of the barley harvest. Ruth decided to go and get some food for herself and her mother-in-law Naomi. After the harvesters had cut and stacked the barley, she went into the field to pick up the little bits of barley they had left.

The field she was working in belonged to a rich man, called Boaz, who was related to the dead husband of Naomi. He saw Ruth picking up these little bits and liked her very much. He said to his servants, "Pull out some good pieces of barley from where you've stacked it. Let the pieces fall into the field, so that this woman can pick them. And don't try to stop her."

He told her she could also drink the water that the men-servants had brought. She was grateful and bowed before him and thanked him. He said, "I've heard all that you've done for Naomi, and I'm sure God will bless you for it." And when it was time to eat, she shared Boaz's bread and wine.

Ruth didn't eat and drink all he gave her, but took some back for Naomi. When Naomi heard her story, she was happy. She said to Ruth, "You must find out where Boaz

sleeps, and then creep up to his feet and lie there tonight."

That night, Ruth washed, put on her best robe, and then found out where Boaz was sleeping. He was near a threshing floor. She crept up to him and lay down. He awoke, saw her and again said what a good person she was. "In the morning," he said, "I'll find another relative of Naomi, who may want to buy her land. He may also be willing to be a husband to you." And when the morning came, he gave her more barley to take back to her mother-in-law.

But the other relative didn't want to buy Naomi's land or to marry Ruth. And this made Boaz happy, for *he* bought the land and married Ruth. They had a baby called Obed, and Naomi looked after him as if he were her own son. Obed had a son called Jesse, and Jesse was the father of David, who later became king of all Israel.

Ruth 1, 2 and 3.

Hannah's Baby Boy

There was a woman called Hannah who had no children but desperately longed for a son. She prayed to God, promising that if he gave her a baby boy, she would make sure he served God all his life. Soon after, she gave birth to a son, and called him Samuel.

She remembered her promise. As soon as Samuel could eat real food, she and her husband took him to a priest called Eli. Eli lived in Shiloh, in a house where people worshiped God. (This house was called a temple.) Hannah left Samuel with Eli, who said he would teach the boy to serve God.

Eli was a good man, but his own sons, were really bad. Although they too were priests, they didn't care about their work. God liked the boy Samuel more than the sons of Eli.

I Samuel 1, 9–28; I Samuel 2, 12 and 26.

God Speaks to Young Samuel

Eli was a priest, and the people used to worship God by bringing him meat which was cooked in front of an altar. The wicked sons of Eli would take the best pieces of meat and eat them themselves. They would take a three-pronged fork and stick it into the pan in which God's meat was being cooked. Whatever stuck on the end of the fork, the sons of Eli ate. But God saw what they were doing and didn't like it. He also thought Eli should have stopped them.

As Eli grew older, his eyesight became weak so that he could hardly see. One day he was lying in the house of God, not quite asleep, when God called out, "Samuel, Samuel." Samuel, who was nearby, heard and thought that Eli was calling him, so he ran up to the old priest and said, "Here I am." Eli said, "I didn't call you. Go back to sleep."

God called Samuel a second time. Again, Samuel thought

it was Eli calling and ran to the priest. But Eli said, "I didn't call you. Go and lie down." When the same thing happened a third time, Eli knew that it must be God calling Samuel. He told Samuel that next time it happened, Samuel was to reply, "Speak to me, God, for your servant is listening."

So Samuel did as Eli had told him. God said, "This is my message. I am going to punish the sons of Eli for their evil ways. They have said bad things about me, and Eli didn't stop them. You must tell Eli what I have told you."

Samuel didn't want to tell the old priest what God had said, but Eli said he wanted to know even it it was hurtful.

Later on, when Eli's sons were killed in battle, everyone realized that Samuel must be a prophet – a person who spoke for God. Soon Samuel was to give people many other messages from God. That was what a prophet did.

I Samuel 2, 13–17; I Samuel 3.

Saul Becomes King

Samuel was a judge as well as a prophet. He would travel from place to place putting right the problems of the Israelites. Eventually he grew too old. His sons became judges too. But they were no good. They would tell lies if people paid them money to do so. So they were always on the side of the rich, even if the rich were doing wrong things.

The Israelites didn't like this. They saw that the other tribes in Canaan were ruled by kings. They came to Samuel and said, "Find us a king." Samuel knew that God didn't really want them to have a king. God was their king. And in any case, all the kings in Canaan were greedy men. Everybody had to serve them. They took the best donkeys, the best fields, the best olives and wines. People's daughters had to cook for them. Others had to fight for them, run ahead of their chariots, making everyone bow down to the kings.

The kings treated most people as slaves. Samuel knew that if any Israelites were to become king, they would be no better.

As usual, the Israelites wouldn't listen to Samuel. So God said, "All right. Find them a king. It's the only way to teach them." God then helped Samuel to find the best king possible. He chose Saul from the land of Benjamin.

At this time Saul was looking all over the country for some donkeys his father had lost. He could not find them; but he was running out of money and food and decided that he ought to go home. To make sure he didn't get lost, he went to ask Samuel the way. Instead of showing him the way, Samuel gave him a splendid meal. Next day he poured a drop of oil on Saul's head and said, "This means God has chosen you to be king of the Israelites."

Samuel now called the Israelites to a place called Mizpah. He still said they were foolish to want a king instead of trusting God to look after them. But since they insisted on having a king, they must choose one. They chose Saul, and then shouted, "Long live the king."

Samuel said that now they had a king he was no longer going to be a judge. At first Saul seemed to rule well. He and his son Jonathan, whom everbody loved, beat off all those who attacked the Israelites.

Soon it became clear that Saul was fighting battles not because God wanted him to protect the Israelites but because he himself was greedy for the sheep, cows and oxen of the other kings and tribes. Soon his own son began to disobey him. Saul would have killed Jonathan, but the people wouldn't let him, because Jonathan had fought bravely.

Samuel felt sorry for Saul; but he refused to see him again. And God was angry that he had made Saul king. He decided that someone else, a young shepherd boy called David, was going to be king instead.

I Samuel 7, 15–16; I Samuel 8 to 14.

David and Goliath

I Samuel 17.

When Saul was king over the children of Israel, their chief enemy was a group of people called the Philistines. One day, the armies of the children of Israel and the Philistines faced each other on either side of a valley, ready to fight.

Suddenly, a huge man, bigger than anyone they had ever seen, strode forward from the Philistines' side and stood in the valley. His name was Goliath. He wore a shining brass helmet and was armed with metal clothing. He shouted that he would fight anyone in the Israelite army. If he won, then they would have to be slaves to the Philistines, but if the Israelite won, then the Philistines would give in.

The Israelites were terrified. Twice a day for forty days he challenged the Israelites, daring anyone to fight him.

Three brothers in the Israelite army had a young brother called David. He was a shepherd. Sometimes a lion might attack his flock. David would chase after it, and kill the lion with his sling.

One day David's father sent him with food for his three brothers in the Israelite army. As David reached the battlefield, Goliath appeared and again dared anyone to fight him. Everyone fled – except David. The Israelites were amazed that he wasn't afraid and decided to take him to King Saul. David offered to fight Goliath. Saul had promised that anyone killing Goliath could marry his daughter and would be made very rich. But David only thought about God's promises to bless the children of Israel.

When Saul heard about the lions David had killed, he agreed that the boy should be allowed to fight Goliath. Saul was so pleased that he even loaned David his own armor. But David was so young that he could hardly walk in it. The armor was too big and heavy. So David just wore his ordinary clothes.

He picked up his shepherd's staff and his sling. As he went out to fight Goliath, he crossed a stream and there he picked up five smooth stones, which he put in his bag.

Goliath laughed out loud at the sight of David. He was sure he could kill an unarmed lad. But David knew that God doesn't simply side with all big people, so he felt quite brave. As Goliath rushed at him, David put one of the stones in his sling and hurled it at the giant. The stone hit Goliath on the forehead, and he fell to the ground. David had no sword, so he ran up to the fallen giant, took away his sword and with it cut off Goliath's head.

The Philistines ran away and the Israelites chased after them, and David went back to King Saul.

David and King Saul

King Saul pretended to be pleased with David, but secretly he was jealous of him because he thought the people liked David better. So Saul played tricks on David.

First, he promised that David could marry his elder daughter Merab. Then, without telling David, he let her marry someone else. Happily, Saul's second daughter was in love with David, so she married him instead.

Next, Saul made David lead the battles against the Philistines, secretly hoping that David would be killed.

Saul had now become a very strange man. Sometimes he was in a bad temper. On some of those days, David used to come and play the harp to the king.

David's playing used to calm Saul, but not always. One day, while David was playing his harp for the king, Saul suddenly stood up, and using all his strength, threw his spear at David. Quickly David leaped out of the way and ran from the king's palace into hiding.

King Saul had a son, Jonathan, who was David's special friend. Jonathan talked to King Saul, reminding him how David had killed Goliath and saved them all. Saul calmed down and was sorry that he had been so angry. David came out of hiding, but still he wasn't safe.

One day, Saul decided to kill David while he was asleep. David's wife, Michal, learned of the plot. She said, "Unless you escape tonight, you'll be dead tomorrow." She helped David escape through the window, and made the bed look as though he was fast asleep in it. Saul's men came to take David away, but she said, "He is ill." Saul was happy, because he thought it was going to be so easy to kill David. He said, "Bring him to me on the bed." When the men told him that

the bed contained a dummy, Saul was angry with Michal. But she said that David would have killed her, if she hadn't helped him to escape.

David secretly came back to see Jonathan. "What shall I do?" asked David. Jonathan replied, "On the day of the full moon, hide behind the stone of Ezel. I will come with a servant for target practice and will shoot some arrows. If I say to my servant, 'Go and fetch my arrows. They are on this side of the stone', you will know you are safe. If I say the arrows are beyond the stone, run for your life."

The next day Jonathan questioned his father. Saul said he hated David and wanted to kill him. Sadly Jonathan went to the field with his servant and shot some arrows. He shouted to the servant, "Go and fetch my arrows. They are beyond the stone." So David knew he had to flee.

David stayed with the prophet Samuel in some huts, and all the prophets protected him. If anyone came near to kill David, the prophets would twirl and dance around them until the killers didn't know what they were doing.

I Samuel 16, 18, 19, 20, 24, 26, 31; II Samuel 1.

David Becomes King

Although Saul behaved badly to David, David would never harm Saul. Once David crept into Saul's tent when Saul was asleep. He could have killed him there and then, but he didn't. Instead he took Saul's spear and the jar of water next to Saul and left with them. When Saul woke up, he knew that David had been there and had spared his life.

In the end, Saul killed himself. The Philistines had killed his sons in a battle, including David's friend Jonathan. Saul was already wounded. The Philistines were about to catch him, but he wasn't going to let them get their hands on him. He stuck his sword into the ground with the blade pointing upwards. Then he fell onto it.

David was very sorry that Saul was dead and even sorrier that Jonathan was dead too. He sang a beautiful sad song for them. All the people liked David now and wanted him to be their king. When he was king, he soon beat the Philistines.

David was very kind to Jonathan's son Mephibosheth. He was crippled badly. David gave him all Saul's goods and allowed him to eat at the king's table for the rest of his life.

David decided that the Israelites needed a chief city where their king could live. The most beautiful city was Jerusalem.

Any enemy would find it hard to capture Jerusalem. But when David first saw it, Jerusalem belonged to people called Jebusites. They said David would never take it from them. But David had a clever plan. He sent some of his bravest men up a water pipe that led into the city. Here they struck down the Jebusites. David rewarded one of the men who had carried out this daring plan by making him a commander. His name was Joab.

David protected Jerusalem by a great wall with huge gates. Then he announced that Jerusalem was to be the chief place for worshiping God.

David was a good king, and protected those who served him. For instance, one very hot day David and his army were trying to capture the city of Bethlehem from the Philistines. David wiped his brow and said to himself, "I wish I could have a drink of water from the well that is just outside Bethlehem." Three of his strongest soldiers heard him, forced their way through the Philistines to the well, and brought back some water for their king. But David was sorry when they gave it to him. "God, stop me from doing this sort of thing," he prayed. "These men could have died to get me some water." Instead of drinking the water, he poured it on the ground and said, "Let this water be only for God."

I Samuel 26 and 31; II Samuel 1, 17–27; II Samuel 5, 1–5 and 17–25; II Samuel 9; I Chronicles 11, 4–9 and 12–19.

David Takes the Ark to Jerusalem

Jerusalem was now the chief place for worshiping God, so David decided that the ark must go there too. He built a special place for it in the middle of the city.

At that time the ark was in Baalah in Judah. The Levites, the people who were specially entrusted to look after the ark, put it on a new cart which was carried by oxen. People went in front and behind it, playing music, dancing and singing. But as they reached a threshing floor, the oxen stumbled. The ark tilted sideways. A man called Uzzah put out his hand to steady it; and as he touched the ark, he fell down dead.

Everybody was alarmed. They felt certain that Uzzah had died because only the Levites were supposed to touch the ark. They thought God was angry. David too was frightened. He decided not to take the ark into Jerusalem after all. He told the Levites to take it to the home of a man called Obed-edom.

There he left it.

But really God wanted to bless any place where his ark was properly looked after. For three months the ark stayed with Obed-edom, and during that time many good things happened not only to him but to all his family. David's courage returned and finally he decided to take the ark into Jerusalem.

On the way to Jerusalem he worshiped God by burning a dead ox and a plump sheep after every six steps taken by the oxen pulling the ark. And as they reached the city David danced in front of the ark. He gave every single person in the city a loaf of bread, some dates and a cake. Everyone was happy, except for David's wife, Michal, who didn't think that a king should behave this way. "You look so silly," she said. But David didn't care. "I was dancing for God," he said. "Why shouldn't I be happy and dance for joy before the God who has made me king of all these people?"

II Samuel 6; I Chronicles 15.

84

David and Bathsheba

David could sometimes be bad. Once, when he was walking on the flat roof of his palace, he saw a very beautiful woman who was washing herself. She was called Bathsheba. David fell in love with her. But she was already married.

Her husband, Uriah, was away in David's army, so the king persuaded Bathsheba to come and live with him. One day, Bathsheba discovered she was going to have a baby. She was frightened that Uriah would find out about David.

David decided to bring Uriah home to live with his wife again. Maybe then Uriah would think that the baby was his. But Uriah thought it wrong to be with her when all the other soldiers were fighting their enemies.

So David decided on a wicked plan. He ordered his commander Joab always to put Uriah where the fighting was the most dangerous. And one day, when the Israelite army was trying to fight its way into a city, a woman dropped a millstone from the ramparts on Uriah, which killed him.

David could now take Bathsheba into his home without fear. But he had made God angry. God sent a prophet called Nathan to tell David how badly he had behaved.

Nathan was a very clever prophet. His plan was to make David himself say how wicked he had been. So he told the king a story. "There was once a rich man who had many sheep. In the same town lived a poor man who had only one little lamb; but he loved this little lamb like a daughter. The greedy rich man stole it from him."

Angrily, David said, "God should kill such a man." "Well," replied Nathan, "you are just like that man."

Realizing what Nathan meant, David told God he was truly sorry for what he had done, so God did not kill him. But when Bathsheba's baby was born, it died after seven days.

II Samuel 11 and 12, 1–23.

Wise King Solomon

David and Bathsheba did have another baby boy. They called him Solomon, and he became king after David. When David died, Zadok the priest and Nathan the prophet put Solomon on King David's own donkey. Then Zadok poured oil over Solomon's head, to show he was the new king. And all the people shouted, "Long live King Solomon!"

Solomon was a very wise king. He loved and served God properly almost all the time. He was also clever enough to marry one of the daughters of an Egyptian Pharaoh, which stopped the Egyptians attacking his land.

The new king was very young and didn't know whether or not he would make a good king. One day he had a dream in which God asked him what he wanted. Solomon didn't ask for lots of money. He just said, "Make me clever enough to tell my people the right things to do and always to judge properly when there are problems between them." To this God replied, "I'll make you cleverer than any king that has ever been. And because you were not greedy and didn't ask for money, I'll make you richer too than any king has ever been. And if you obey me, I'll let you live a long time."

Here is one of the cleverest things that Solomon ever did. Two women came to him with a baby. These women lived in the same house, and both had had baby boys who looked like each other. But one night, one of the babies died.

His mother was cunning. While the other woman slept, she changed the babies around, giving the dead baby to the sleeping mother. But when this mother woke up, she looked carefully at the dead boy and saw it wasn't her child.

How was she to prove this? The mother who had stolen the living baby swore that it was hers. So they went to Solomon.

Solomon heard the tale of each woman, and he thought of a trick to find out which was really the mother of the child. He said, "Bring a sword and cut the baby in two. Each mother can have half a child."

Now the real mother was terribly afraid for her son. She loved him so much that she would rather lose him than see him killed. She said quickly, "Please don't kill him. Give him to this other woman before you do that." But the other woman simply said, "Cut him in two."

Solomon saw all this. He said, "Don't kill the baby. Give him to the woman who would have given him away rather than see him killed. She is his mother."

Everyone was amazed at such wisdom. In fact, Solomon was so wise that people came from all over the world to ask him questions. Even kings and queens came. The queen of Sheba was so pleased when he answered all her questions that she gave him all kinds of presents.

II Samuel 12, 12–25; I Kings 2, 38–40; I Kings 3 and 10.

Solomon Builds a Temple in Jerusalem

Since the ark of God was now in Jerusalem, Solomon decided to build an enormous, beautiful Temple for it. David had wanted to build one, but God wouldn't let him do so. He wanted that joy to belong to his son, Solomon.

Because God had made Solomon very rich, he was able to build the most wonderful house for the ark.

Inside Solomon's Temple were many rooms, each with a window, and right in the middle was a room for the ark, which they called 'the holy of holies'.

Solomon used all kinds of wood to decorate the Temple – there was wood from fir and cedar trees as well as olive and palm trees. There were carvings everywhere. Inside this beautiful Temple were golden candlesticks and shining lamps. The altar was made of gold, and some of the hinges on the doors were also of gold.

The wise king also employed a famous bronze worker called Hiram to work in the temple. Hiram made huge pillars of bronze, and bronze lions and bulls, and huge basins for holding water. He decorated the temple with bronze pomegranates. It was magnificent.

Finally, the ark was placed inside the newly built Temple. For a time a great cloud filled the whole building, so that nobody could do or see anything inside it. And then Solomon

thanked God for all he had done for the Israelites. He prayed for himself, for the Israelites, and for anyone else who came to pray in God's Temple in Jerusalem. Even if they weren't Israelites, Solomon asked God to bless them.

For the next seven days they all worshiped God. During these seven days they burned twenty-two thousand oxen and a hundred and twenty thousand sheep in the worship of God.

I Kings 5, 15–18; I Kings 6 and 7, 13–51; I Kings 8.

Elijah on Mount Carmel

After Solomon died, no king was strong enough to rule all the Israelites. They were divided into two kingdoms, one called Israel, in the north, the other called Judah. Many of their kings were bad men and worshipped not God but Baal. A very bad king, called Ahab, married a foreign queen, called Jezebel, who tried to kill all God's prophets and brought to Israel four hundred prophets of Baal.

One brave prophet of God, called Elijah, wasn't afraid even though Ahab often tried to hurt him. He assembled all the people on Mount Carmel. And he said, "Get two bulls. Put one of them on the altar for Baal. And I'll put one on an altar for God. But don't set fire to the wood on the altar. We shall see whether Baal or God can do that."

There were two hundred and fifty prophets of Baal, but only Elijah to speak for God. All that morning the two

hundred and fifty prophets called on Baal to light the wood. Nothing happened. Elijah was laughing at them. "Maybe Baal has gone to sleep; I'm sure he will soon wake up," he jeered. "Or perhaps he is away on a long journey." The prophets of Baal became so angry at this that they began to cut themselves with spears and swords to try to make Baal do something. Still nothing happened.

Now it was Elijah's turn. He said to all the people, "Come closer to me." His altar had twelve great stones, to remind them of the twelve Israelite tribes. He poured water over the wood, to make it even harder to set it on fire. He dug a trench around his altar and filled that with water too. And then he prayed to God. God not only lit the fire and burned up the bull and the wood, but also steamed away all the water.

Then everyone fell to the ground, shouting praise to God. And Elijah killed every prophet of Baal in Israel.

I Kings 11, 41–43; I Kings 18.

Elijah and Queen Jezebel

Jezebel was always making King Ahab do bad things. She had brought the prophets of Baal to Israel. Now she made the king greedy. And Elijah didn't like any of this.

Near the king's house, a poor man called Naboth had a field in which he grew vines. Ahab wanted to buy this field from Naboth, and turn it into a vegetable garden. But Naboth's relatives from long ago had grown vines in that field. He refused to sell it. He didn't even want to change it for a better field.

Ahab was very sad because he had really wanted the field. So when he returned to the palace he sulked in his room and refused to see anybody or to eat anything. Eventually, Jezebel went to see what was the matter. He explained that even though he had offered Naboth a better vineyard and more money than the vineyard was worth, he still did not want to sell. "Are you not king of Israel?" sneered Jezebel.

"Get up; I'll get the field for you."

So Jezebel arranged for Naboth to be killed. Two men were paid to lie and say that Naboth had said evil things about God and the king. When people heard, they threw stones at Naboth, and killed him. Then Jezebel told her husband Ahab that he was free to take Naboth's field of vines.

Elijah heard of all this from God. Jezebel had already tried to kill Elijah because he had outwitted the prophets of Baal on Mount Carmel. Elijah fled to the wilderness. God sent messengers to feed him. He told Elijah to find a great fighter called Jehu. Then he was to tell everyone that Jehu was to be king, instead of Ahab.

Now Elijah came to Ahab and Jezebel and told them they would both soon be killed for what they had done to Naboth. Elijah added that dogs would eat Jezebel's dead body. Ahab went into battle and he was killed.

I Kings 19, 1–18; I Kings 21; I Kings 22, 29–38.

Elisha Takes Over from Elijah

A warrior called Jehu then decided it was time to take over as king of Israel. He drove in his chariot, at the head of his army, to Jezreel, where Jezebel was. On the way there he killed Ahab's son. Jezebel appeared at her window wearing finery, to be pleasing to Jehu. But two servants who hated her threw her out of the window. Jehu drove over her. When people came to bury her, they found that the dogs had eaten her just as Elijah had foretold.

Elijah was tired and wanted to die; but God gave him strength because there was more work for Elijah to do. He said that the next great prophet would be called Elisha.

Elijah found Elisha plowing a field. To show that he was to be the next prophet, Elijah took off his coat and put it round Elisha's shoulders. When he had done this God sent a chariot of fire, pulled by horses of fire. Elijah got in, and a whirlwind carried him away. Elisha kept Elijah's coat.

Elisha did marvelous things, with God's help. Once he found a spring that gave bad water. He threw salt in it, and the water became immediately clean. Another time he met an old widow, with two children, who had no money or food. A man to whom she owed money was going to take her children away and make them work for him for nothing. Elisha gave the widow some oil which didn't run out for days. She had enough oil to pay the man what she owed him and live on the rest.

Another time Elisha was staying with a family whose son had died. Elisha stretched out over him and he became alive.

Just like Elijah, Elisha helped anyone who had a problem, whether that person was important or not. Once the commander of the Syrian army, Naaman, fell ill. He had leprosy. His wife had a little girl servant who was an Israelite. She told Naaman's wife that her husband ought to go to see if Elisha could cure him.

Elisha had heard all about this and wrote to the king of Syria saying, "Send Naaman to me." The king, who badly wanted Naaman to get better, gave lots of money to the king of Israel so that Naaman could pass safely through the country. (At first the king of Israel thought the king of Syria was making fun of him. How could anyone cure Naaman?) Naaman traveled through the country safely and arrived at Elisha's house in his chariot. Elisha didn't even bother to come out to see him. He just sent a message: "Bathe seven times in the river Jordan and you'll get better."

At first Naaman was puzzled and angry. "I'm not going to do that," he said. "It's silly. I can bathe in any river I want to." However, his servants said, "Please do as Elisha says." So Naaman bathed in the river Jordan and came out healed. It was foolish not to listen to a prophet of God.

II Kings 9, 14–37; I Kings 19, 19–21; II Kings 2, 4 and 5.

Amos, the Shepherd-Prophet

Many people grew angry with what the prophets were telling them. They just didn't want to listen any more. What good did it do them?

There was one prophet called Amos. He was a shepherd and lived in Judah. God told him to go to Israel and speak to the people there. Amos told them that if they didn't mend their ways they would soon lose the land God had given them. Nobody liked that message. They drove him back into Judah. "We don't want you here," they said, "telling us that things are bad."

Amos didn't like the way the Israelites treated the poor. God meant them to help people in need. Instead, they trampled on them. So Amos said that the kind of thing that happened to the evil Pharaoh at the time of Moses could happen to them. Locusts would come and eat their crops.

Amos believed that one day God might even destroy the Temple built by Solomon. He told the people that he had seen God standing at the side of the altar, and God had said, "Smash down the pillars and let the roof fall in." But God's news was not all bad. Amos also believed that God still wanted good things to come to the children of Israel. Once they had given up their evil ways, he would build things up again. If they could learn to do what God wanted, life would be even better. It would be as if once they had planted a crop, it would grow healthily and quickly. People would say that there were so many good grapes on the mountain that wine flowed down the mountainsides.

So although God, through Amos, told the Israelites that they would certainly be punished for their wicked ways, he also gave them something to hope for after their punishment.

Amos 5, 7, 8 and 9.

The Loving Prophet Hosea

In the past, God had managed to make even the bad people turn to him and start being good. At the time of Amos, God also spoke through another prophet called Hosea.

Hosea was married. But his wife ran away from him, leaving him with their three children – two boys and a girl. Hosea called his children odd names, because he wanted people to learn from these names about God. His first boy was called Jezreel, to remind them of all that had happened during the time of Ahab and Jezebel. His daughter was called "Not loved," because God couldn't go on loving the evil children of Israel. His second son he called "Not-my-people", because God would not necessarily go on for ever calling the children of Israel his special people.

Even though Hosea felt hurt when his wife left him, he still loved her and managed to persuade her to come back. He thought, "This is how God sees the children of Israel. Even if

they desert him for false gods, he still wants them back."

This didn't mean they could go on behaving as badly as before. Hosea knew that the priests who still burned animals to God didn't please him unless they obeyed all his rules as well. He knew that the present kings of the Israelites had shown themselves to be wicked, because by this time the Israelites were even using the same Temple at Jerusalem to worship both God and false gods like Baal. Hosea warned them that this was wrong. "I knew that a king would be bad for you," said God. "Your kings have simply made you more wicked than before. Now I will get rid of them."

The people hated to hear all this. "Hosea is mad," they said. "He is out of his mind." But Hosea was right. God would soon have the Israelites thrown out of the promised land. But because he loved them so much, just as Hosea loved his wife, he would one day let them back again.

Hosea 1 to 3; 5, 1–7; 9, 7–9; 11 and 13, 9–11.

The Call of Isaiah

Elijah and Elisha both lived most of their lives in the northern kingdom of Israel. But God didn't forget to send prophets to the southern kingdom, which was called Judah. He helped the kings of Judah whenever anyone tried to attack them.

Because Jerusalem was in Judah, one of God's prophets, Isaiah, spent much of his time in Solomon's Temple there. One day he was standing near the altar when he saw God sitting high up on a throne. His robe filled the whole sanctuary. Isaiah was overcome. Around God were wonderful beings called seraphs, each with six wings. They covered their faces with two of their wings; they covered their feet with two more; and with the other two they flew. And they sang to each other, "God is pure and has no time for bad things. His greatness is found everywhere in the world."

It seemed to Isaiah that as they sang, Solomon's Temple almost fell down. He was really frightened now. God was perfect. Isaiah wasn't. He said, "O God, I am scared. I've seen you, but I'm a bad man." God sent one of the seraphs with a lighted piece of coal from the altar, which he held in a pair of tongs. The burning coal touched Isaiah's lips, but it didn't burn him. The seraph said, "Now you are pure. This fire has made you pure."

God then told Isaiah to tell the people of Judah to follow his rules, or everything in their lives would go wrong.

So Isaiah told the children of Israel again and again that it only needed a few Israelites to disobey God, for all Israelites to suffer. If the children of Israel disobeyed God, then God would let other nations, such as the Assyrians, defeat the Israelites in battle. Then there would only be a few good Israelites left, like the only good bit of an old torn cloth.

Isaiah 6; Isaiah 10 and 11.

The Suffering Prophet Jeremiah

The prophets had to tell people what God wanted and not what the people wanted to hear. Since they couldn't attack God, the people would attack his prophets instead.

This was Jeremiah's problem. He was a prophet living near Jerusalem. Jeremiah could see that other nations were now stronger than the Israelites. Also God was no longer pleased with his people and was planning to punish them. Jeremiah kept warning, "God wants you to go back to him." He told them all that they must stop telling lies.

They didn't listen. First their king Josiah was killed by an Egyptian Pharaoh. Josiah's son became king; but the Pharaoh soon captured him and forced the Israelites to pay lots of money to Egypt. Then Nebuchadnezzar, king of Babylon, started attacking the Israelites. Jeremiah tried all sorts of ways to make them understand that God was not pleased with them. Once he took a pot and broke it in front of a lot of Israelites. "God will break this nation in the same way," he said. Another time, he put ropes and an animal's harness on his neck. "God will let other people use you like animals," he said. But they refused to pay attention.

One king, called Zedekiah, tried to fight back against Nebuchadnezzar. But because Zedekiah didn't bother to obey God's rules, God didn't help him. Even so, Zedekiah did ask Jeremiah to pray to God for the Israelites.

Jeremiah would not do this. He knew that soon Israel would be defeated whatever he did. Instead, he decided to go home and divide his land up between his relatives. As he was leaving Jerusalem, a soldier asked, "Where are you going? Are you going to join our enemies?" Jeremiah answered, "No." But they didn't believe him. They beat him and jailed him in an underground cell.

II Kings 23, 28–30; Jeremiah 3; 4, 1–4; 27; and 37, 1–16.

Jeremiah in the Cistern

After a while, King Zedekiah realized that Jeremiah was not a fool but spoke for God. So he sent for him secretly and asked whether God had anything to say to the children of Israel.

Jeremiah said that God's message was that they would soon be ruled by the king of Babylon. Jeremiah also told the king that putting him in prison was unfair. He didn't tell lies. Zedekiah agreed and sent Jeremiah to live with the king's guards, who fed him.

Jeremiah's troubles weren't over yet. He couldn't help telling people what God intended to happen. Jeremiah said that Jerusalem would certainly be captured by its enemies. Anyone who stayed inside the city would be killed. The rest would be taken prisoner.

Some of the leaders of the city heard the prophet saying this. They complained to King Zedekiah. Jeremiah, they said, was upsetting everyone. The king told them to do what they wanted with Jeremiah. So they threw him down a deep cistern. There was no water in this cistern, only mud.

Now a man called Ebed-melech told the king this was wrong. Jeremiah had done no harm. If he stayed in the mud, he was sure to die. The king thought about this and agreed. So Ebed-melech had Jeremiah pulled out gently. Old rags and worn-out clothes were put under his arms, so that he wouldn't be hurt by the ropes they used to get him out.

Then Zedekiah and Jeremiah had a last meeting. In secret, Jeremiah told the king that the best plan was to give in to his enemies. Then he would not be killed. Jeremiah made the king promise not to tell anyone of their conversation, for he didn't want to be thrown down the cistern again because his words upset people. Then he went to stay in the place where the guards lived, until Jerusalem was captured.

Jeremiah 37, 10–21; and 38.

The Israelites are Exiled

Everything happened as the prophets said it would. Nebuchadnezzar, who was king of Babylon, brought a huge army to attack Jerusalem. The city was surrounded for nearly four months. After a while, those inside had no food at all. Then Nebuchadnezzar's army broke down part of the city wall. The king of Jerusalem ran away, but he was captured. And many Israelite leaders were killed.

Then the Temple built by Solomon was utterly destroyed. Nebuchadnezzar's army smashed the great bronze pillars. They took away the golden bowls, the great basins and the wonderful silver candlesticks. They stole the splendid golden bulls and pomegranates.

They forced four thousand six hundred people to leave their homes to go and live in Babylon. There they sang sad songs. "By the rivers of Babylon we were crying," they sang, "especially when we remembered Jerusalem. The lovely gold of our Temple is no longer gleaming. The stones of our fine buildings are now scattered at the street corners." Soon the people gave up singing altogether, they were so sad.

But they still prayed to God. They asked him to start loving them again, and to take them home. There were still prophets living with them. One, called Ezekiel, spent most of his life in Babylon. He had loved the Temple, where he had been a priest as a young man. He told them that one day God would give a new spirit to all the Israelites. He would even join together Judah and Israel again.

Ezekiel used to tell stories to the exiles. One of his most marvelous was a description of how they would live again as God's people. God, Ezekiel said, took him away to a great valley filled with dry bones. Ezekiel walked among them all.

Then God said to him, "Speak on my behalf to these bones. Tell them I am going to bring them to life. Tell them I shall cover them with skin and give them muscles and blood.

And they will all know that I am God."

As Ezekiel did this, there was a clattering. It was all the bones coming together. He looked again, and they all had muscles. Skin was growing over them. God said, "Tell the winds to blow breath into them." And suddenly all the bones stood up. They were alive. They were like a huge army.

God said to Ezekiel, "These bones are all the Israelites. They are like dead bones. They think there is no hope for them. But tell them that I, God, will give them life again and settle them in their own land. And I shall be their God for ever."

Ezekiel 37, 40, 41 and 42; Jeremiah 39 and 52; Psalm 137; Lamentations 4 and 5.

The Fiery Furnace

Nebuchadnezzar wanted to get some of the exiles from Judah to work for him. He told one of his chief servants to find good-looking, strong men who were also intelligent. They would be trained for three years, fed from the king's food, and then be part of Nebuchadnezzar's staff.

Three of these young men were named by their captors Shadrach, Meshach and Abednego. But even with these new names they never forgot that they were the servants of God.

Their problems began when Nebuchadnezzar decided to make a huge golden model of a god, and ordered everybody to worship it. Each day music would be played. As soon as the people heard the music, they had to bow down to the ground and worship the golden model god. If they refused, they would be thrown into a great blazing fire.

By this time Shadrach, Meshach and Abednego were trusted rulers of parts of Nebuchadnezzar's land. But people saw that they didn't bow down whenever the music of the golden model god was played. Nebuchadnezzar ordered the three young men to come to the palace. "If you won't bow down to this golden god," he said, "you'll be thrown into the blazing fire. Your God won't save you then." They replied, "Maybe he will save us. Maybe he will not. But whatever happens we won't bow down to the golden god."

Nebuchadnezzar was terribly angry. He said. "Heat up the fire seven times hotter than usual." The three young men were tied up and thrown into it. In fact, the fire was so hot, it burned up those who threw the young men into it. But it didn't hurt Shadrach, Meshach and Abednego at all. They walked about in it, singing a song in praise of God. They sang that everything should praise God: the stars, animals, men and women, everyone and everything should praise God who saved them from the terrible fire. And God's messenger walked about with them in the flames, looking after them.

King Nebuchadnezzar sprang to his feet in amazement and shouted, "Shadrach, Meshach and Abednego, servants of the most, high, God, come out." The fire had had no effect on their bodies. Not even a hair on their head was burned. And Nebuchadnezzar decreed, "Let anyone speak badly of Shadrach, Meshach and Abednego and I will have him torn limb from limb and his house burned to the ground, for there is no other God that can save like this." And after that the king treated them well for the rest of their lives.

Daniel 1, 3–8; and 3.

Daniel in the Lion Pit

Another of the young men from the children of Israel brought to the court of Nebuchadnezzar was called Daniel. All went well for Daniel during the reigns of Nebuchadnezzar and of Belshazzar. These two kings were followed by one called Darius.

Darius liked Daniel and gave him a lot of power. Some people grew jealous of this and worked out a way of getting Daniel into trouble. Daniel was a good man who worshiped God and never did anything wrong. But his enemies told King Darius to make a new law, stopping people asking favors of anyone except the king for thirty days. This meant that people couldn't ask favors of God in their prayers and if anyone disobeyed this law, they were to be put to death.

Now Daniel's enemies knew he wouldn't stop praying, so they watched him. Three times a day he continued to open his window, face towards Jerusalem and bow down in praise to God. The men who hated Daniel told Darius he was asking favors of his God. Darius was upset (he hadn't seen through their evil plans). He thought carefully of ways to save Daniel, but he didn't dare go against his own law. In the end he said to Daniel, "I have no choice but to have you thrown into a

lion pit. Your God will have to save you."

So Daniel was thrown into the lion pit and a great stone was put over the pit. The king went back to his house and was so upset that he couldn't sleep that night.

First thing in the morning, the king rushed to the lion pit. "Daniel," he shouted, "are you all right? Has God looked after you?" Daniel shouted back, "Yes. God sent a messenger, who kept all the lions' mouths shut. So I've not been hurt." The king was relieved. He had Daniel pulled out of the pit and the men who had made trouble for Daniel were thrown in. Before they reached the bottom of the pit, the hungry lions tore them to pieces.

After that, Darius made things go even better for Daniel. He even told everyone how wonderful Daniel's God was.

Daniel 6.

Rebuilding Solomon's Temple

Some of the kings who had beaten the Israelites in battle were kind to them. One of these was Cyrus, king of Persia. By the time he became king, the Israelites had lived outside the promised land for fifty years. Cyrus told them that if they wished, they could go back to Jerusalem to rebuild the Temple.

This made many of them very happy. Cyrus even gave back the cups and other temple treasures which Nebuchadnezzar had taken from Solomon's Temple. He gave them thirty golden bowls, a thousand and twenty-nine silver bowls, and a thousand other bowls, jugs and basins which had come from the old temple.

Many of the exiles returned home. They gave money to other people who lived in the promised land, and they brought new cedar wood from Lebanon. But even before they built a new Temple, they started worshiping God again in the ruins of the old one. They set up the altar in its old spot. There they burned animals just as they had done long before. They began to keep the feasts Moses had ordered, especially the feast of the Passover. Most people were happy. But some of the old people, who remembered how beautiful Solomon's Temple had been, were in tears. So there was a strange mixture: some shouting with happiness because they were back home, others crying because the Temple was in ruins.

Of course, some of the exiles' enemies in Canaan were not pleased. The people who lived in Samaria, even tried to stop them from rebuilding the Temple. They wrote to the rulers who had taken the people of Judah (the Jews) captive, asking them to stop the building. But the people wouldn't stop.

And when the new Temple was finished, they went wild with happiness. They burned many animals in praise of God. They burned a hundred bulls, two hundred rams, four hundred lambs and twelve goats – a goat for each of the twelve tribes. By burning these goats each tribe was saying it was sorry for upsetting God.

A man called Nehemiah, looked after the wine of King Artaxerxes, far away from Jerusalem. One day the king saw that Nehemiah was looking very sad. He asked why. Nehemiah told him that he was sad because although a beautiful new Temple had been built in Jerusalem, the city itself was still in ruins. Its walls had been pulled down. Its great gates had been set on fire.

Artaxerxes said that Nehemiah should go back to Jerusalem to try to put things right. So Nehemiah set out for Jerusalem. He went around the city, looking at the ruined gates in the ruined walls. When he saw them, he was sad. He told the people to collect money so they could rebuild the city.

Again the enemies of the Jews would have stopped the work if they could. But the builders divided themselves into two groups. From that time on, only half of them did the building. The other half stood on guard, in case someone came to try to stop the work. They had spears and shields and bows and armor. Everyone else worked until dark, to make sure that the walls were finished as quickly as possible.

Thousands of exiles returned home. People were now calling them Jews (that is, people who came from Judah). A prophet called Ezra decided to remind them of all the things they had learned over the many years away. He took a book in which were written the rules that Moses had given them. And he read them aloud. It took from early morning until midday to finish reading the list. And then he cried, "God is a great God." Everyone bowed down.

Still some people were sad. But Ezra told them not to be. It was a great time for them. So they went home and drank and ate, thanking God for everything.

Ezra 1, 3, 4 and 6, 14–18; Nehemiah 2 to 4 and 8, 1–12.

Job in Trouble

By now the Jews knew that they would be in trouble if they didn't obey God's rules. But was that the only reason for being good? Were people only good and kind because that meant God would be good and kind to them? Or should they be good and kind whatever happened to them?

God tried to show that they must be good whatever happens. There was a man called Job who lived in the land of Uz far away from Canaan. He worshiped God. He never did anything wrong. All went well with him. He was very rich. He had seven thousand sheep, three thousand camels, a thousand oxen and five hundred donkeys. He had many servants, and many happy sons and daughters.

One of God's servants pointed out that no one knew why Job was so good. "He doesn't do it for nothing," said the servant, who had some wicked ways. "He does it because you reward him. Take away all that Job possesses, and he will hate you." God replied, "As a test, you can do whatever you like to Job, provided you don't harm him."

This servant of God then made dreadful things happen to Job. First, his enemies stole his oxen and his donkeys. Then his sheep were burned to death. Next his servants were killed. And lastly, and most tragically, his sons and daughters were killed.

Did Job hate God after this? Job got up, and though he was almost despairing, he said, "When I was born, I had nothing. When I die, I shall have nothing. God gives and God takes away things from us. We must worship him whatever he does, and however he does it."

God's servant wasn't pleased. He had hoped to show that Job would hate God. He said to God, "I know why Job still loves you. You won't let me harm him personally. He is still fit and well." God answered, "Don't kill Job; but do anything else you want to him. We'll see whether or not he really loves me."

So God's servant struck Job with boils and ulcers all over his skin. Job tried to scrape them off. He sat in an ashpit and was very miserable. But when his wife said, "It's time you started hating God, because of all the things he has let happen to you." Job replied, "Don't be foolish. Whatever God lets happen to us, we should still worship him." Job still wouldn't do anything wrong.

Job never understood why sometimes things went wrong and sometimes they went well. But he wouldn't hate God. And in the end God did give him back his happiness and his goods again. He had seven more sons and three more daughters. (He called the girls Turtledove, Cassia and Mascara.) And by the time he died, an old and happy man, he had fourteen thousand sheep, six thousand camels, two thousand oxen and one thousand donkeys.

Job 1, 2 and 42, 10–17.

Esther in Persia

As the Jews in Babylon had found out, it was sometimes dangerous not to live in their own land. The Jews who settled in a land called Persia found this out too.

In a town called Susa lived a beautiful Jewish girl called Esther. After her parents died, her uncle Mordecai brought her up as his own daughter. Mordecai was a trusted servant of the king of Persia. He sent Esther to work in the palace, telling her not to say she was Jewish. The king soon found what a lovely person she was. In fact, he loved her so much that he married her and made her his queen.

One of the king's chief servants, called Haman, hated the Jews. He didn't like them having their own rules, and he was jealous of men like Mordecai. He hated Jews so much that he promised to give the king a lot of money if the king would order the deaths of all Jews. Not knowing that his wife Esther

was a Jewish girl, the king agreed.

Esther decided she must save her people. She would make the king change his mind. She prayed to God for several days. Then she put on her most beautiful clothing and went to see her husband. She was very frightened, because she and all her people might soon be killed. She almost fainted with fear but she talked to the king. He told Esther he would do anything for her. She invited the king and Haman to a special dinner. At this meal Esther said, "There is a man who wants to kill me and all my people." The king asked, "Who is this dreadful man?" – and Esther pointed to Haman.

The king was outraged at Haman's cruel plans. "Hang Haman where he planned to hang Mordecai," he ordered. So the evil death Haman planned for a kind Jew happened to Haman instead. And all the Jews of Persia were saved.

Esther 2 to 6.

Jonah Tries to Run from God

By now the Jews had spent a lot of time with other tribes. They had to ask themselves what God really thought about these other people. Some of them believed that God must hate the other tribes, but this wasn't true.

Once God told a prophet called Jonah to go and give messages to the people who lived in the city of Nineveh. Jonah didn't want to do this, so he tried to run away from God. He boarded a ship that was going to a distant place called Tarshish, believing that God couldn't possibly follow him there.

God decided to teach Jonah a lesson. He arranged for a great storm. Jonah was asleep in the ship. The other sailors started praying to their gods, hoping they wouldn't sink. To make the ship lighter so that it would float more easily, they threw their goods overboard.

Suddenly one of them found Jonah under a blanket fast

asleep, and wondered why he wasn't praying to his God. Some of the other sailors asked themselves why they were having such bad luck. Perhaps, they said, one person on board was unlucky. It could be his fault that there was such a terrible storm. "Perhaps," they said, "it's Jonah's fault."

Jonah himself thought this might be true, because he knew that he must have annoyed God by running away instead of going to Nineveh to tell the people there that God wanted them to be good. God had said, "I feel sorry for Nineveh. There are a hundred and twenty thousand people living there who know nothing about living good lives. There are lots of animals there as well, and I like them too."

So Jonah told the sailors, "The best thing to do is throw me overboard as you did with the goods that were making the ship heavy." He knew that God would look after him. And of course God did.

Jonah 1, 1–13; *Jonah 4*, 11.

Jonah Overboard

The sailors decided to pray to God asking him not to punish them for what they were going to do. Then overboard Jonah went, and the sea grew calm again.

God had a strange adventure waiting for Jonah. As soon as he fell into the sea, a huge fish swallowed him alive. Inside the fish he could do nothing but say prayers. After three days the fish vomited him up onto the beach.

Jonah found that he was near Nineveh. Now he had no choice but to do what God had asked him to do in the first place. He went to Nineveh and told the people that if they didn't start being good, they would be punished. They listened and decided to try to live better lives, so God didn't punish them. Jonah learned that God loved other people as well as the Jews.

Jonah 1, 14–16; Jonah 2 and 3.

THE NEW TESTAMENT

Mary's Good News

A young woman called Mary was planning to marry a man called Joseph. They both lived in Galilee, in a small town called Nazareth. Nearby, in a town in the hills, lived Mary's friend Elizabeth and her husband Zechariah, a priest in the Temple. Elizabeth and Zechariah were much older than Mary.

One day, it was Zechariah's turn to go to the Temple to light some fragrant spices, round the altar, so that sweet-smelling smoke could fill the Temple. Suddenly he saw a strange person standing in the smoke to the right of the altar. Poor Zechariah was terribly frightened; but this strange person told him not to be afraid. "My name is Gabriel," said the visitor. "I have come from God with good news." The good news was that Zechariah and Elizabeth were to have a baby son. Because Zechariah would not believe what he had heard he was struck dumb. The people in the Temple were wondering why he was hidden near the altar for so long. But when he came out to them, all he could do was make signs. His voice did not come back until the baby was born.

Six months later this same Gabriel visited Mary, as she was sitting alone one day, "Greetings Mary. The Lord is with you and has greatly blessed you. Do not be afraid. You are to have a son. And you must call him Jesus. He will be great. He will be known as the Son of God and he will rule over the people of Israel for ever."

Mary was astonished. "I can't have a baby," she said. "I'm still a virgin." But Gabriel said she was not to be afraid, for the spirit of God could do everything. "I am God's servant," said Mary. "Let whatever God wants happen to me."

As quickly as she could, she went to see Elizabeth. When Mary came in, Elizabeth felt her baby leap for joy inside her. Elizabeth said how wonderful that Mary should be the mother of this baby who was going to be everyone's Lord.

Mary was so happy that she began to sing. She sang about

how she was a nobody, but God had chosen her and no one else to have this special baby.

People would remember her for ever. But, she sang, all this was due to God, who all the time makes little people great, and feeds hungry people and makes them more important than the mighty people of the world. God had always promised to do this, from as far back as the time of Abraham. Now God had done the same for her.

Luke 1, 25–56.

No Room at the Inn

The Roman emperor, Caesar Augustus, decided to make a list of everyone living in his lands. In order to do this, he told everyone to go back to the place where they had been born. Their names, along with the names of their children, would be put on a list. In this way Caesar Augustus would know how many people he ruled.

Mary and Joseph lived in Nazareth, but Joseph was a descendant of the great King David and had been born in David's city, Bethlehem. So Joseph and Mary went there. When Joseph and Mary reached Bethlehem, they looked for a place to stay, but couldn't find anything. Mary was ready to have her baby. At last Joseph found a place for the baby to be born – this was a stable. There was straw on the floor, and it was in this place that Jesus was born. Mary wrapped him up warmly, and put him in a manger because this was safe.

Jesus was born in David's city because God wanted everyone to know that Jesus was to be a great king too. He was born in a stable so that the poor would think that Jesus was on their side.

Luke 2, 1–7.

Jesus is Visited

On the night that Jesus was born, God sent his messenger to some shepherds who were looking after their flocks on the hillsides outside Bethlehem. "Don't be afraid," the messenger said.

"Everyone must be happy. Today in Bethlehem a baby has been born.

Through him God will show himself to the world."
God's messenger told the shepherds that they would find him lying in a manger in a stable.

Suddenly the skies were full of many of God's servants, all loudly singing:

*"Let everyone in heaven worship God,
and all those whom God loves shall live in peace."*
Then the messengers disappeared.

The shepherds were amazed. They looked at each other. And then they all rushed off to Bethlehem to see the baby called Jesus.

Then God sent a message to some wise men who lived east of Jerusalem. They saw a great star in the sky, shining clear and bright. They said, "This star must belong to a very great person. We must follow it."

Then they read some words written by the prophet Micah. He wrote that in Bethlehem one of the greatest leaders of the children of Israel would be born. So they went to Bethlehem. The great star was over their heads.

They found the baby Jesus with his mother Mary and Joseph. The wise men brought with them gifts of gold, frankincense and myrrh which they gave to Jesus. And the wise men returned home. The shepherds returned to their flocks praising God for all that they had heard and seen.

So although Jesus was born in a humble stable, this didn't mean that he was of no importance. God wanted to show the

whole world that his little child was very important – Jesus
cared about poor people like the shepherds and rich ones like
the wise men.

Matthew 2, 1–2 and 9–12; Luke 2, 8–20.

Hiding the Baby from Herod

On their way to see Jesus, the wise men were invited by Herod the Great, King of Judea to visit him. He was frightened that someone else would want to be king and kill him. He said "Tell me where this new baby is. I will go and worship him." He really wanted to kill Jesus.

God told the wise men to tell Herod nothing. After they had visited Jesus in Bethlehem the wise men returned home by a different route. Herod was furious. He decided he would kill *every* boy baby.

God sent a messenger to Joseph, telling him what Herod planned to do. The messenger said Joseph must take Mary and the baby away into Egypt. They set off that very night, and stayed in Egypt away from danger.

Then Herod did a terrible thing. He killed every boy baby he could find, under two years old, who lived in Bethlehem or near it.

Soon after this, Herod died. God's messenger went to Joseph in Egypt and told him he could go back home. But Joseph knew that Herod's son, Archelaus, was now king. He might be as cruel as his father.

So Joseph didn't go anywhere near Bethlehem. He went back to Galilee, where he and Mary had lived before Jesus was born. There they lived, in a little town called Nazareth. And that is why later on people called Jesus a Nazarene, because he came from Nazareth.

Matthew 2, 3–8 and 12–22.

127

Jesus as a Boy in the Temple

Mary and Joseph obeyed all the rules which God gave to Moses. Because they lived near to Jerusalem, they could keep the feast of the Passover in the Temple itself. They went there each year, with many other people.

Jesus didn't go with them to the Temple in Jerusalem until he was twelve. By then everyone could see that God was blessing him.

Mary and Joseph were proud to take Jesus with them to Jerusalem. After the feast was over, they set off home. Mary and Joseph thought Jesus was with their friends among the great many people in the group of travelers. But he wasn't. After three days, Mary and Joseph discovered this, and they were very worried. They couldn't find Jesus anywhere. So they returned to Jerusalem and looked for him everywhere.

At last they came to the Temple. There was Jesus, sitting

with the wisest of all the men who looked after the Temple. He was listening to what they had to say, asking them questions, learning from them. They were all astonished that Jesus knew so much.

Mary said to him, "My son, Why have you behaved like this? We've been so worried about you." Jesus answered, "I thought you would know that I was here in the Temple, doing the work of my father."

When he spoke of his father, he didn't mean Joseph. He meant God. Neither Joseph nor Mary knew what he meant. But Mary remembered it all, and thought about Jesus's words.

Jesus went back home with them to Nazareth. He grew up and he learned more and more. He was loved by everybody.

Luke 2, 39–52.

Jesus is Baptized

Jesus had a friend called John. He was the son of Mary's cousin Elizabeth. When John grew up he decided to go and live in the desert, near the river Jordan. He dressed in hairy camel-skins and lived on honey made by wild bees. He also ate strange desert vegetables.

He did this because he was angry with people who didn't keep God's rules. A lot of people listened when he said this. They decided to become better people and try to live their lives obeying God. John would tell soldiers not to force people to give them extra money and goods, just because they were stronger than others. To people who collected money for the government, John would say, "Never take more than you should." To everybody he said, "If you have two coats and see somebody who has none, give him one."

Those people who agreed with John asked him how they could show God that they had changed. John told them to go to the river. He poured water over them, and it was just as if the bad things they had done were washed away.

The people called this "baptism". John became known as John the Baptist. Some people even thought that he was God's greatest prophet, but John knew that the greatest prophet of all was Jesus. He told everyone this.

One day John was very surprised to see Jesus coming to him, wanting to be baptized. John said, "You should be baptizing me." Jesus knew that God liked what John was doing. Jesus wanted to show people that he was pleased as well and wanted everyone else to be baptized.

So John baptized Jesus. When Jesus came up from the river, he saw God's spirit coming down to him. It looked like a beautiful dove. And God's voice said, "You are my son, the one I love above all. I will always bless you."

Matthew 3; Luke 3, 1–18 and 21–22; Mark 1, 1–11.

The Devil Tries to Tempt Jesus

Jesus next decided to spend a lot of time thinking what he should do to obey his father in heaven. For forty days and forty nights he lived in the desert, all the time asking himself how he could best do his father's work on earth. He knew there were many wild beasts in the desert. But he also knew that God's special messengers would take care of him.

For these forty days and nights he ate nothing, because there was nothing there to eat. And he wanted to prove that God would look after him.

Soon he was very hungry. Now this was the chance for an evil being, called the devil, to trick Jesus, if he could, into doing something wrong. The devil knew that Jesus could do anything, for God was always with him to help him. So the devil cunningly said, "There are a lot of stones here. Why don't you just make them into loaves of bread?"

Before replying, Jesus thought long and hard about all the things God had shown to the children of Israel through Moses. Jesus was in the desert where Moses had spent forty years leading the Israelites to the promised land. He remembered that long ago God had fed the children of Israel with manna because God hadn't wanted the children of Israel to spend all their time thinking about food and nothing else. He would give them food for their bodies. But he also had much more to give them. He would give them his rules, which would make their lives happier and better.

So Jesus told the devil, "We don't only live by eating bread. We live as well by everything that God tells us."

The devil had to think of another way to tempt Jesus to do something wrong. He said, "Imagine that you are standing high up on the Temple wall, in Jerusalem. You could show everyone how great you are by throwing yourself over the ledge." Then the devil said, "God will certainly send his messengers to catch you. You won't come to any harm."

Jesus remembered that when Moses was leading the children of Israel through the desert, they made God very angry by always grumbling and saying, "Is God on our side or not?" Moses had told them, "Stop trying to test your God." Now Jesus said the same thing to the devil.

The devil cunningly tried once more to make Jesus do something wrong. "Why not be on my side?" he said. "I could give you everything in the world." But Jesus knew that to be on the devil's side meant to do the exact opposite of God's rules. He said, "We must worship only one God and do what he wants us to do."

The devil had tried his hardest to make Jesus do wrong, but he couldn't, and so he went away. Then God's messengers came back to look after Jesus.

Exodus 17, 1–7; Deuteronomy 6, 13 and 16; Deuteronomy 8, 3; Matthew 4, 1–11; Mark 1, 12–13; Luke 4.

John the Baptist is Killed

John the Baptist was very brave. He even told the kings to stop being bad. One of these was called Herod, not the king who had tried to kill Jesus when he was a baby.

Herod had stolen his own brother's wife and married her himself. John the Baptist said this was wrong. So Herod and his wife, Herodias, had John chained up in a prison. She wanted to kill John. But Herod knew John was a good man and was too frightened to kill him.

One day, Herodias found a way to kill John. As it was Herod's birthday, he was giving himself a huge party – for the important people and for the leaders of the army.

Herodias's daughter could dance splendidly. Her mother said, "Dance for your father and his guests. If he offers you a present, come to me. I'll tell you what to ask for."

So Herodias's daughter danced and Herod was very
pleased. In front of everyone, he promised to give her any
present she asked for. She rushed to her mother, who said,
"Ask him for the head of John the Baptist on a big plate."

This was horrible, but Herodias's daughter asked for it.
Herod was upset, but he didn't dare go back on his promise
because everyone was watching him. He sent a bodyguard to
the prison, telling him to bring back John's head.

So in prison John's head was cut off. Herod gave it to
Herodias's daughter. She gave it to her mother.

John the Baptist's friends came to the prison and took his
body. They buried it and came to tell Jesus what had
happened. Jesus was very sad. He got into a boat and sailed to
a remote place, where he could be alone.

Matthew 14, 3–13; Mark 6, 17–29; Luke 3, 19–20.

Jesus Finds Some Helpers

When John the Baptist was put into prison, Jesus decided he needed some helpers in the work God had planned for him.

He began to go about telling everyone that he had good news from God. If they would listen and stop being wicked, then God would soon make everything right with the world.

Jesus taught everywhere, sometimes in the open-air, sometimes in the synagogues where the people worshiped. One day he was by a lake, talking to a huge crowd, when he spotted some fishermen washing their nets. The man in charge was called Simon.

Jesus borrowed their boat, and they sailed out a little way on the lake, so that the crowd could see and hear him better. Then Jesus decided to make Simon and his brother Andrew give up fishing and become his first helpers.

He said he would show them how to do great things. "Let's set out to sea and catch some more fish," he said. Simon and

Andrew had caught nothing all night. Even so, they obeyed Jesus. This time they caught so many fish that they had to get help from two other fishermen in another boat. By the time they pulled in all their fishing nets, the boats were so filled with fish that they almost sank.

Simon knelt before Jesus when he saw this. "I'm not good enough to be with you," he said. "I'm too wicked." Jesus answered, "Don't be frightened. You must follow me everywhere. From now on you won't catch fish. I'll show you how to catch people."

So Simon and Andrew became the first two people that Jesus chose to help him in his work. Straight away they were joined by the two men from the other boat. They were also brothers, called James and John, sons of Zebedee.

Matthew 4, 17–22; Mark 1, 14–20; Luke 4, 14 and 5, 1–12.

More Helpers for Jesus

Soon Jesus found more helpers. There were twelve special ones who went everywhere with him. These included the fishermen Simon, Andrew, James and John. Then there were women who looked after him whenever he came to their towns. There were children, who were his friends. And there were people who wanted to be his friends, but were too scared to say so – because Jesus had so many enemies.

Whenever he found a new friend, Jesus helped him to grow into a better person. Sometimes silly people would see him sitting with those whose lives had been bad. They would say, "Look at Jesus. He shouldn't be with those bad people. Perhaps he doesn't know how wicked they have been." But Jesus would answer, "You are wrong. I'm like a doctor who makes sick people better again. I'm here to teach bad people to be good."

One man who was helped by Jesus was Levi. Levi collected money for taxes. Jesus told him to give up that job and follow him. Levi was very happy because he really wanted to lead a better life. He gave a big party for his new master, Jesus. Then Levi left his tax office to start a new life as a friend of Jesus. He decided to show that he had changed by taking a new name, and afterwards everyone called him Matthew.

Jesus also changed the name of Simon, the first of all his helpers. It happened like this. Many people wondered who Jesus was. Some thought he might be John the Baptist, come alive again. Some thought he was the prophet Elijah, come back to earth or any number of other prophets. One day Jesus said to his friends and helpers, "Who do *you* think I am?"

Simon spoke up and said, "You are the person we have all been waiting for. You are God's specially chosen one. You are God's son."

"You are a happy man, Simon. My father in heaven must have told you this," said Jesus.

Then Jesus changed Simon's name to Peter, which means rock. Jesus said to him, "You are Peter, you are a rock. You are the rock on which I will build my church. It will be so strong that nothing will harm my friends who stand on it. All my helpers from now on will rest on this rock."

Of course, Jesus's helpers, even Peter, did not always do good things or keep God's rules. But they always tried to do so, and Jesus was always helping them and teaching them to be better by looking after others.

Sometimes, for instance, his helpers became greedy. Once James and John, Zebedee's sons, came up to him and asked Jesus to let them have the most important positions in his group of helpers. They wanted to sit next to him on the day to come when all the world would say Jesus is king. Their mother had persuaded them to ask for these places. The other disciples were very angry because James and John wanted to be treated better than anyone else. But Jesus told them that there was no way in which he could give them the best places. Friends and helpers of Jesus had first of all to look after other people before looking after themselves.

Matthew 9, 9–13; 10, 2–4; 16, 13–20; 20, 20–28; Mark 2, 13–17; 3, 16–19; 8, 27–30; 10, 35–45; Luke 5, 27–32; 6, 14–16; 19, 18–21; John 1, 40–49; 3.

Jesus Preaches from a Hill

Sometimes Jesus taught many people in huge crowds. Sometimes he wanted to tell things to his closest friends.

One day he left the crowds and went to the top of a hill. There he sat down and waited for his disciples. When they came, he told them who were the happiest people:

"Happy people are those who don't have much power or too much money. They have God in their hearts.
Happy people are gentle.
Happy people are kind and forgiving.
Happy people have pure hearts. God looks after all these.
Even people who are sad can be happy, for God will put all evil and sad things right.
Even people who are hated by wicked men and women

can be happy. God will look after them.

People who make peace are happy. That's what God's children should do.

Those who long to see all wicked things done away with are happy. God will give them all their wishes."

Then Jesus reminded his friends how people in the past had been nasty to the prophets, though these prophets had told the people God's messages. "If people treat you like that," he said, "you can still be happy. God will give you a great reward for being true to him." And he told them that they were like salt on food. If the salt is no good, the food won't taste good. He also said that his friends and helpers were like great lights, shining in the world to let people see the truth.

Matthew 5, 1–16.

Jesus Teaches a Prayer

Sitting on the hillside, Jesus told his friends that none of the rules of God were to be broken.

He said this did not mean that people could just keep all the rules and then think everything was all right. What mattered with God was what a person really thought.

Moses had told the children of Israel that God would not allow them to murder anyone. Jesus said, "Even if you don't murder anyone because you're afraid of being caught and punished, that doesn't mean you are a good person. It's wrong even to wish you could murder someone. It's wrong to hate anyone at all, even if that person really hates you."

Jesus said that his friends should always be ready to look after other people. Sometimes this might mean giving away something precious. "Don't turn away anyone in need," he said, "do even more than they ask."

He also told them not to do good things hoping that other people will notice. It isn't what other people think that matters. What matters is what God thinks about us. So, Jesus said, if we want to give away some money, we should give it away secretly. God will know what we have done.

Then Jesus told his friends a prayer to say to God:
"Our father who art in heaven,
Hallowed by Thy name.
Thy kingdom come, Thy will be done,
On earth as it is in heaven.
Give us this day our daily bread;
And forgive us our debts, as we forgive our debtors;
And lead us not into temptation, but deliver us from
  evil.
For Thine is the kingdom, and the power,
  and glory forever."

Matthew 5, 17–48; Matthew 6, 1–18; Luke 11, 2–4.

Jesus the Storyteller

Jesus loved talking to people. He would talk to them in boats, in the fields, in towns, in the synagogues and at parties.

He told them things about children. He said anyone who harms a child would be punished by God. He told them it was silly to want too much money. A person with too much money would have as much difficulty getting into God's kingdom as a camel getting through the eye of a needle.

But most of all, Jesus told people stories. He thought that the best way of telling about God and God's good news.

Sometimes the stories were funny. He told of silly people who bring lamps to light their bedrooms and then hide them under the bed. When he wanted to tell people to keep on praying, whatever happened to them, he said that such a person praying was like a man knocking on the door of a friend who is in bed in the middle of the night. Knock and knock, and soon he is bound to get out of bed even if he doesn't want to.

He told stories about shepherds and vines and workmen. He told them about clever men, and about people saying their prayers. He told them about hidden treasure, and about fish nets full of good fish mixed up with garbage. He told stories about judges and widows and fig trees without any figs.

Sometimes people didn't try to understand what he was saying. Jesus then said, "Some people have ears, but they're too silly to use them." But he went on trying to get through to them.

Matthew 13, 1–3 and 44–51; 18, 5; 19, 23–26; Mark 4, 1–2 and 21; 9, 42; Luke 11, 5–9; 16, 1–8; 18, 1–14 and 24–27; 21, 29–33.

The Story of the Two Sons

Jesus told a story about the two sons of a rich farmer. One decided he didn't want to work anymore. He just wanted a good time. He asked his father to give him everything that would be his when the father died.

The father was very sad that his son was so foolish. But he let him have his share of the family's goods. A few days later, the son left home.

Far away, he simply wasted all of his money enjoying himself. Soon he had nothing left. He had to find some work to earn enough to eat. Food in that faraway land cost a lot, because there was very little of it. The son of the rich farmer found work looking after pigs. He was so poor and hungry that even the pigs were better fed than he was. He would look at them hungrily, wishing he could eat their food.

In the end he thought, "I'll go back home. My father's servants have enough to eat. Maybe he'll let me join them."

Now his father had longed for the son to come back home. He was always looking out for him. So he saw his son when he was still a long way off. He still loved him very much. He ran to meet him and threw his arms around him and kissed him.

The son said, "I'm no longer good enough to be one of your sons. Let me work for you as a servant." But his father wouldn't have that. He put the best clothes he could find on the son. He put a ring on his finger. He gave him new shoes. And he made his servants cook a lovely fat calf. Then they all had a feast.

They were already dancing merrily and playing music when the son's elder brother came in from working in the fields. He was upset. He said to his father, "I've always obeyed you. You never gave such a party for me." The father explained why he was wrong. He said, "You know that one day you will have everything that belongs to me. You are loved by me too. But we must be happy because your brother is back. When he went away, it was as if he had died. Now he is back, and it is as if he has come back to life again. We have found the son we had lost."

So Jesus tried to teach people to love and forgive those who have been silly but have come back to their senses. This, he said, is how God treats us.

Luke 5, 11–22.

The Good Man from Samaria

Sometimes Jesus told stories to answer other people's questions. Once Jesus and another man were talking about the rules given by God through Moses.

Now Jesus thought the two greatest rules were these:

"Love God as much as you possibly can;

Love your neighbor as much as you love yourself."

On this occasion the other man asked Jesus, "Who is my neighbor?" To make him understand, Jesus told a story about a man who was going on a dangerous journey from Jerusalem to a place called Jericho. Some thieves caught him. They beat him up. They robbed him of everything he had, and left him nearly dead.

Soon a priest came along. He saw the poor man lying there, but he didn't care. And even though he was a priest, he crossed over to the other side of the road, so he could pass the man without bothering to help.

Another religious man came along, but he too crossed over
to the other side and went on without helping the poor man.

And last came a man from Samaria. Usually people from
Samaria and Jews disliked each other. But as soon as he saw
the Jew lying nearly dead, he stopped. He put ointment and
bandages on his wounds. He lifted the man onto his own
donkey and took him to the next village, where there was an
inn. There the sick man could be looked after. But the man
from Samaria did more than this. He gave money to the
person who owned the inn for looking after the sick man.

Then the man from Samaria said, "If it costs you any more
to look after him, next time I'm here I'll pay it."

When Jesus had finished telling that story, everyone knew
who had been a good neighbor and who had been a bad
neighbor to the man beaten up by the thieves.

*Leviticus 19, 18; Deuteronomy 6, 5; Matthew 22, 34–40; Mark
12, 28–34.*

147

The Good Shepherd

Jesus knew that people wondered who he was. How could he explain to them? And what was the best way of telling them what he wanted them to do?

A good way was to use pictures and stories about their daily lives, and then use these examples to show how God worked and how he wanted good men and women to behave.

Jesus used to say he was like a shepherd to all his friends. Bad shepherds ran off if a dangerous animal came near. That left the sheep helpless and the wild animals could then attack and scatter them. At other times, a bad shepherd would fall asleep and forget about his sheep, and other people would come and steal them.

Jesus was like a good shepherd. A good shepherd could

recognize all his sheep, because they belonged to him. He had many sheep, all over the land, and he wanted them to live in peace with each other. If the sheep were in danger, he would even be prepared to die to protect them.

Jesus cared for his friends in that way. And he wanted all sorts of people to become his friends, so that everyone could live in peace together. He wanted his friends to trust him to look after them, as sheep can trust a good shepherd.

He also knew that sheep – and people – can sometimes behave badly. What happened if a man had a hundred sheep and one of them went astray and got lost on a dangerous mountain? A good man would leave his ninety-nine good sheep safely looked after and go out over the mountainside to bring back the sheep that was lost.

Jesus wanted people to see that God is like this. One bad person who starts obeying God's rules again makes God very happy. He is like a lost sheep who has been found.

Matthew 18, 12–14; *Luke 15,* 4–7; *John 10.*

149

The Rich Man and Poor Lazarus

Jesus said it was silly to want too much money. Money makes no difference to God.

Nobody, he said, however rich, could make himself look more beautiful than the tiniest things God had made. He told people to look at the lovely birds and gorgeous animals. Not even Solomon with all his wealth had been able to dress in clothes finer or more beautiful than birds' feathers or animals' fur.

Jesus told people that God loves everyone equally, rich and poor, humble and great. He told them a story about a man who grew vines and needed some people to help him. In the morning he went out and found some helpers. "I'll pay you a penny a day," he said. They agreed and started work at once. All day he kept finding other people who had no work. He sent them all to look after his vines with the other workers.

At the end of the day, said Jesus, he paid them all a penny. Those who started work first got only the same pay as those who started last. The ones who had done most work said this wasn't fair. But Jesus wasn't really talking about earning money. He was saying that God loves and cares just as much for those who can do a lot as for those who can do a little.

Jesus also said that God, can be very angry with rich people who don't care about the poor. Another of his stories was about a rich man who dressed in fine clothes and every day had a great feast. But he never cared about a poor man called Lazarus, who lay at the door of his house. Lazarus was very ill. Dogs came and licked his sores. But he knew that the rich man's table was so filled with food that scraps often fell to the ground. How this poor beggar longed to eat those scraps.

Eventually, the rich man and poor Lazarus both died. In heaven, Abraham put his arms round Lazarus and made him happy. But the rich man, who had done nothing to help poor Lazarus, was taken to a place where the flames never die out.

He called out to Abraham, pleading with him to send Lazarus with a drop of water. "That is impossible," replied Abraham. "You had all your good things on earth. Lazarus had nothing. Now all is changed. Between us and you is a great gulf to prevent anyone from crossing from your side to ours or from our side to yours."

The rich man then wanted Abraham to send Lazarus to tell his greedy brothers what was going to happen to them. But Abraham said no. He knew that even if somebody came from the dead to warn the brothers, they were so greedy they still wouldn't change their way of life.

Matthew 6, 25–34; 20, 1–16; Luke 12, 22–31; 16, 19–31.

The Wicked Servants

In the past, the children of Israel had killed prophets sent from God, because they didn't want to hear God's messages. Jesus knew that this might happen to him too.

He told a story to show that he knew this. It was about a man who planted many vines. He built a wall round them. Then he paid others to work in the field for him.

When all the grapes were ripe, he sent servants to collect them. But the wicked people working there beat up one servant, killed another and threw great stones at a third.

The man who owned the vines thought, "I'll send my son to gather the grapes. The workers won't kill him." But they did.

Many Jews thought they were like a field of vines planted by God. God wanted them to do good things, the way a man who owns vines wants them to give good grapes. But these

people also knew that they often did bad things. Some of them didn't care, so long as they had all the good things of life for themselves.

So when Jesus told the story of the wicked workers and the vines, some of the leaders of the people knew he was really talking about them. When Jesus talked about the workers killing the man's son, some of the people became very angry. They thought perhaps that Jesus was saying that *he* was God's son.

They didn't like this story. When they heard it, they wanted to put Jesus into prison. But many others liked Jesus very much and were willing to learn from him. By now they thought he was a prophet, and they wouldn't let anyone arrest him.

Isaiah 5; Matthew 21, 33–46; Mark 12, 1–12; Luke 20, 9–19; John 8, 37.

The Great Wedding Feast

Long before Jesus was born, prophets had sometimes said they would have to punish people who didn't obey God's rules.

Amos had said that people who swindled, and people who cruelly treated the poor would find out that God didn't like them. "You won't be having feasts," God said. "Every day will be like a funeral. Instead of singing, you'll be crying."

Amos had even said that God would stop treating the children of Israel as his own people if they did not remember his rules and obey them.

Some of this had already happened. The children of Israel never forgot what had happened to them when Nebuchanezzar destroyed their Temple, taking them as prisoners to Babylon. Then they had sung sad songs, asking God to forgive them. They sang:

"God, don't forget what has happened to us;
  look at us, see how miserable we are.

Other people now own what used to be ours;
  they even live in our homes.

Make us come back to you, God, and we will come;
  let the old happy days come back."

One of Jesus' stories made people remember all this. It was about a king who gave a wedding party for his son. But the people he had invited didn't care about the king or his son. They were like those children of Israel who hadn't cared about God's kindnesses to them.

In Jesus' story, even when the king sent his servants to remind people of the wedding, they still wouldn't come. They made silly excuses. Some of them even killed the king's servants or beat them.

The king was furious. He sent his soldiers to punish those who had ill-treated his servants. And he ordered the servants to bring all sorts of other people to the wedding. If they were poor or crippled, blind or lame, that didn't matter. They should all come.

It didn't matter if those who came to the wedding feast had once been bad people. But once they had come to the wedding, they must show they were grateful.

In those days, wedding guests wore a special wedding dress. It was very rude not to wear one. Jesus ended his story with the king seeing a guest who hadn't put on his special dress. "Tie him up and throw him out," said the king. Jesus wanted to say that people who accepted God's kindnesses but were not grateful for them really hurt God. It showed that they didn't care about God, whatever he did for them.

Amos 8, 4–10; 9, 7–10; Lamentations 5, 1, 2 and 21; Matthew 22, 1–14; Luke 14, 16–24.

The Ten Bridesmaids

Although Jesus didn't approve of greedy people who took more than they should of God's gifts, he liked parties. Some people said he should not always be enjoying life so much with his friends. These miserable people said that John the Baptist had not done this. Who was right? John the Baptist – who told people to pray and eat very little – or Jesus?

Jesus said there were times when people should say their prayers. Sometimes they should be at work in the world. Sometimes they shouldn't eat – maybe for a whole day or more – to show that they were not greedy. Sometimes they should be happy because God had given them so much.

Jesus also loved going to weddings with his mother and his friends. And he liked telling stories about weddings.

One of his stories was this. There were ten bridesmaids who were waiting for a bridegroom. In those days, it was the duty of bridesmaids to wait for the arrival of the bridegroom and look after him before his wedding. In Jesus' story, the bridegroom was late. The bridesmaids didn't know when he would arrive. He might even come during the night. So the bridesmaids all had lamps which burned oil.

Five of these bridesmaids were wise girls. They didn't want to let the bridegroom down. When evening came, they went to sleep with oil in their lamps, ready to light them the moment the bridegroom arrived.

The other five didn't care about the bridegroom. They hadn't even bought enough oil to light their lamps.

Then at midnight there was a sudden shout, "The bridegroom is here. Run out to meet him." The sensible bridesmaids leaped up, lit their lamps and rushed out to greet him. As they were leaving, the stupid bridesmaids said, "Give us some of your oil. We want to light our lamps and come out too." But the wise bridesmaids wouldn't give them any. They needed all their oil to make sure that their lamps didn't go out. They told the others to buy their own oil.

By the time the foolish bridesmaids had got back from buying oil, the wedding had started. The doors were locked. When they tried to get in, the bridegroom wouldn't open them. Since he hadn't even seen them he said "I don't know you."

When he had finished the story, Jesus said, "Be ready all the time." He meant that we never know when God will need us to be prepared to do something important for him. We must be ready to work for God whenever he wants us, always looking out for things to do for him.

Matthew 9, 14–17; 25, 1–13; Mark 2, 18–22; Luke 5, 33–39; 6, 24–26; John 2, 1–10.

157

The Unkind Servant

Jesus told people that it was wrong not to help others. He also said people should forgive those people who were sorry for what they had done wrong.

Jesus knew that God forgave those who had done bad things and then were truly sorry. He knew that when someone had been forgiven by God, he should be ready to forgive others in the same way.

To explain all this, he told a story about a king who decided that all the people who owed him money should pay it back.

One of his servants owed the king a large sum of money. There was no way he could pay it back. The king said the only thing to do was to sell the man and his wife and his children as slaves. He would also take all the money they had.

Miserable and terrified the unfortunate man threw himself at the king's feet. "Please give me time to pay everything," he begged. The king felt sorry for him and said he needn't pay anything.

As the servant was leaving, he came across another man – who was also a servant of the king. This man owed the first servant a small sum of money. But the first servant had already forgotten how kindly the king had treated him. He seized the man by his throat and said he must pay immediately. The man couldn't, so the unkind servant threw him into prison.

Then the king's other servants were upset. They told the king what had happened, and he became really angry. "What a wicked person you are," he told the unkind servant. "Why didn't you let the man off his debt? That's what I did to you." So he threw the unkind servant into prison, and had him tortured until the day he had paid off all the money he owed.

Jesus said, "That is how my heavenly father will deal with you, unless each of you truly forgives his fellow man."

Matthew 18, 23–35.

159

The Story of the Sower

Matthew 13, 4–23; Mark 4, 3–20; Luke 8, 4–15.

Sometimes people did not understand some of Jesus' stories at first. He used to explain them later to his close friends.

This was so with the story he told of a man sowing seeds. The man threw these seeds all over his field. Some of them fell onto the path at the side of the fields. People trampled on these seeds and spoiled them. The birds came and ate them. They never grew.

Other seeds were thrown where there were rocks. The sun soon made them grow up into long stalks. But their roots could not get down into the soil through the rocks, and so the seeds did not have enough water to live. They grew quickly and then died away.

Other seeds fell where there were weeds. These weeds were too strong for the seeds. They grew all over them and killed them.

And some seeds fell onto good ground. These grew strong and healthy. They produced a rich crop of new seeds for the sower to collect and make into bread.

Jesus' friends asked him why he had told this story. So he told them what it meant.

The seeds, he said, stand for God's messages and rules, sent to the earth. The ground stands for different people who hear these messages and rules. Those who hear God's messages and then let evil people or the devil take them out of their hearts are like the hard ground from which the birds take the seeds. Those who seem to be listening to the messages of God and obeying them for a while are like the rocks where the seeds fall. Soon they give up obeying. God's messages die away inside them.

The seeds which fall among weeds remind us of people who love too many good things and too much money. This means that there is no room for God's wishes.

The good ground stands for people who hear God's messages and really listen to them. They obey what God tells them. And then all sorts of good things come from them, giving lots of happiness to others.

Jesus Heals Sick People

Jesus could cure the sick. Soon after he chose Simon as one of his best friends, Simon's mother fell ill. Jesus made her better right away. People soon found this out. They would bring along their friends who suffered all kinds of illnesses, and Jesus would make them well again.

Once a man with a terrible skin disease called leprosy said to him, "If you want to, you can make me well." Jesus answered, "I do want to make you well." He touched the man's skin, saying, "Be cured." And immediately the man's skin was healed.

Jesus did not have time to heal everyone. He had other things to do. He had to pray. He had to tell everyone God's good news. Because of this, he often asked those who had been healed not to tell anyone. But they usually forgot, and hundreds of sick people begged his help.

Some of those he cured grew to love him very much and went around with him, along with his twelve chief helpers. Three of them were Mary Magdalene, a woman called Joanna (whose husband worked for the ruler called Herod), and another called Susanna. When Jesus was in trouble later on, they did all they could to help him.

Mark 1, 29–34 and 40–45; Luke 5, 12–16; 8, 1–3.

Jesus Heals a Paralyzed Man

Some of the people Jesus healed were very sick indeed. But for the help of their friends, they would never have been able to come to him. Sometimes their friends worked hard to bring them to him from distant places.

Once Jesus was in a place called Capernaum near Nazareth, talking to people inside a house. So many men and women wanted to hear Jesus that the place was packed full. People were even standing in a crowd outside the house, longing to hear what Jesus had to tell them but not being able to hear.

Four men had a friend who couldn't move. He was paralyzed and lay on a stretcher. They decided to carry him to Jesus, hoping he would cure him. But they couldn't get their friend through the crowd. They decided to pull him up to the rooftop. Then they stripped off part of the roof and lowered him through the hole they had made to where Jesus was speaking.

Jesus was pleased that the men believed he could cure their friend. He decided to show everyone that he could also forgive anything wrong that the sick man might have done. "Your sins are forgiven," he said to the paralyzed man.

Some people were now angry. They believed only God could forgive sins. They didn't believe that Jesus was God or the son of God.

Knowing what they were thinking, Jesus said it was easy for him to forgive people's sins if they were sorry for them, just as he could also cure their diseases. He turned to the paralyzed man and said, "Stand up. Pick up your stretcher, and go home." The man stood up and walked off while everyone watched. They were amazed, and knew that Jesus healed people and forgave their sins too, because God was with him.

Matthew 9, 1–8; Mark 2, 1–12; Luke 5, 17–26.

The Daughter of Jairus

When he cured sick people, Jesus showed them that God wanted everyone to be well and whole. He showed them what life would be like in God's kingdom and in heaven.

What did God think of those who had died? What did God do for them? Jesus wanted to show that God gives them new life and hope.

The chance to do this came when a man called Jairus went to Jesus for help. Jairus had an important job as an official in a synagogue. He told Jesus that his only daughter was so ill that she was about to die. He begged Jesus to come and save her life.

Jesus hurried on his way to the synagogue house where Jairus lived and where his daughter lay ill. But he was surrounded by a huge crowd of people, all of them wanting him to talk to them and to do things for them. It was hard for him to get through them. They didn't know about Jairus's daughter dying in the house. They had their own problems.

In this crowd was a very poor woman. She had not been able to stop the bleeding inside her for twelve years. She had been to many doctors for all sorts of treatment. Some of the treatment had been painful. She put up with it, hoping to get better. In fact, she only got worse.

She had heard of Jesus' skills. She believed he was so wonderful that if she could touch only a part of his cloak, she would get better. She managed to push her way through the crowd until she was directly behind him. She fell forwards touched his cloak, and was immediately cured.

Jesus knew someone had touched him. He turned around and saw the woman. She was frightened in case he was angry. But Jesus praised her. She had believed in him, and this had made her well.

By now, Jesus had been delayed too long. When he reached

the house by the synagogue, he could hear people playing sad music, because Jairus's daughter had died.

Jesus decided to show everyone what to think of people who have died and are with God. "She isn't dead," he said. "She's asleep." But on hearing this they laughed.

Jesus let only Peter, John and James of his friends, together with Jairus and his wife, go into the house. He took their daughter by the hand and said, "Child, get up." And she got up at once, alive and well. Jesus told her parents to give her something to eat. He ordered them to keep what had happened a secret, but people couldn't help finding out about it. The news spread everywhere.

Matthew 9, 18–26; Mark 5, 21–43; Luke 8, 40–56.

The Grateful Leper

Often people whom Jesus had cured loved him a lot. They were very grateful. But sometimes these people who had been healed didn't seem to care enough even to say thank you. Once they were healed, they soon forgot him. This was true even of the people who had been cured of the most hideous diseases.

Leprosy was one of those diseases. It was a disease that made people look quite horrible. Swellings and scabs and shiny spots appeared on them. Their skin went white. The disease could gradually spread all over them.

When that happened, the person was described as unclean. This was because when Jesus lived, leprosy was believed to be a disease that spread to other people very easily. Nobody wanted to go near a leper. Nobody wanted to touch even a leper's clothing.

Lepers weren't allowed to live with other people. They were forced to wear torn clothes. Everywhere they went, they had to cry out, "Unclean, Unclean," and ring bells so that other people could avoid them.

Any leper who thought he had got better had to go and show himself to a priest. If the priest said he was cured, he was really happy. That was a time to thank God. They would have a special act of worship. They would burn a lamb in praise of God. Sometimes they burned two lambs. Then the healed leper could live as a normal person, meeting friends again.

One day, as Jesus was walking towards Jerusalem with his friends, he passed through a part of the country on the border between Galilee and Samaria. There, just outside a village, were ten people all suffering from leprosy. They didn't come near Jesus because they were unclean, but they shouted to him from afar off, "Jesus, master, have pity on us."

Jesus shouted back to the ten lepers, "Go and show

168

yourselves to some priests." They set off to do so, and as they went, suddenly all of them were cured.

Then one of them turned back. He was so happy that he praised God at the top of his voice. He bowed right down to the ground before Jesus and thanked him.

This man was a Samaritan. Jesus said, "All ten were made clean again. Where are the other nine?" Then he said to his friends, "Only this man from another country has come back to praise God." And to the man he said, "Stand up. Go on your way. You have been saved because you believe in me."

The other nine had been cured of this dreadful illness, but they hadn't bothered to come to Jesus and say thank you. They had been cured by Jesus, but they still didn't believe in him or in what was good and right.

Leviticus 13, 45–59; 14, 1–32; Luke 17, 11–19.

Jesus Makes a Blind Beggar See

In Jerusalem there lived a man who had been blind from the day he was born. All he could do was sit in the street, begging people to give him money or food.

One day Jesus met him. Jesus made a paste with clay and put it on the man's eyes. Then he told the blind beggar to go and wash the clay off in one of the main pools of Jerusalem. The blind man did so, and found he could see.

Some of Jesus' enemies thought they could get him into trouble over this. Jesus had made the paste on the seventh day of the week, when God's rules said everyone should rest. They didn't know God was in Jesus, teaching them to help people in trouble all the time, whether it was the seventh day of the week or not.

What they said was, "He can't come from God if he works on the seventh day." But others said, "How can Jesus be a bad man if he can help people in this wonderful way?"

Next, Jesus' enemies tried to prove he hadn't cured the man at all. They asked the beggar's parents if he had been able to see all the time. The parents were scared. The men who opposed Jesus said they would throw out of the synagogues anyone who liked him. The beggar's parents didn't want this to happen. So they wouldn't tell the truth which was that Jesus had cured their blind son. Instead, they said, "We don't know what happened. He once was blind; now he can see; ask him yourselves who cured him."

Jesus' enemies sent for the beggar again. "Are you going to be a friend of this man Jesus?" they asked. They were very rude. They said, "Jesus doesn't come from God, because he forgets God's rule about resting on the seventh day."

But the beggar replied, "You are stupid. Jesus made me see. He must have come from God." At this, Jesus's enemies were even angrier, and drove the man away.

After he had been driven away, he came back to Jesus and worshiped him. Jesus said, "You can see the truth. There are some people who aren't blind, but they cannot see what you see." So sometimes the good things Jesus did, and the sick people he cured, made his enemies hate him more.

In the end his enemies managed to catch him. And they had Jesus killed, in spite of all the good that he had done. When his friend Peter described Jesus to other people, he said that God gave him his own spirit and power to do good and heal people. Yet people put him to death. It was strange and sad. But that is what happened.

Jesus knew it would happen. And yet he still went on doing as much good as he could.

Matthew 16, 21–23; Mark 8, 31–33; Luke 9, 22; John 9.

Jesus Drives Out a Mad Spirit

There was a very unhappy man whom nobody seemed to be able to help. They said he had a mad spirit inside him. He was very strong, so strong that when people tried to tie him up because of his wild behavior, he always broke free. He could break chains and the iron bands which were put around his arms and legs.

So he was forced to live alone on cliffs at the edge of a lake, close to the tombs where dead people had been buried, in the country of the Gerasenes. All night long, this poor man would scream and cut himself with stones.

Then Jesus arrived. The man saw him in the distance, ran up to him and fell at his feet. He was so mad that he thought even Jesus might torture him. "Swear you won't hurt me," he begged.

Jesus was not like that at all. But the poor man couldn't

even tell him his name. He told Jesus that all sorts of unclean spirits were inside him. Jesus said he could get rid of these spirits. He told the man he would send the spirits out of him into some pigs that were nearby. What happened next was very strange. All the pigs ran over the cliffs into the lake and were drowned.

The pig-keepers ran off into a nearby city and told everyone what had happened. They came back and found Jesus sitting and talking quietly with the man who before had shouted all the time. He was cured.

But the people were afraid because of what had happened to the pigs. They begged Jesus to go away. The cured man wanted to leave with him, but Jesus told him to go home and tell everyone what God had done for him. And everyone who heard of it was astonished.

Matthew 8, 28–34; Mark 5, 1–20; Luke 8, 26–39.

The Wedding Feast at Cana

Sometimes Jesus did things that other people could never do. But this was not to show how great he was. He always had a better reason than that. All the wonderful things he did were like his stories. They had something to teach those who could properly understand the meaning of them.

This was true of the first amazing thing he ever did. It happened at a wedding at a place called Cana. There were so many guests that the wine ran out.

Jesus was there with his twelve chief helpers and his mother Mary. She knew what a wonderful person her son was. But the man in charge of the wedding feast did not know what to do to get more wine and was getting very upset. Mary went to ask Jesus for him.

At that time, Jesus did not wish people to know too much about him. He needed to teach them slowly, so they would learn everything properly at the right time. He decided he

would help the man in charge of the wedding feast, but he would do so in secret. Only Mary, his twelve friends and the servants who served the wine would know what he had done.

Mary told the servants to do exactly whatever Jesus told them. He made them bring six huge pots, each one filled with water. Then Jesus immediately turned all the water into wine. There was much more than would be needed, and no chance of it running out again.

The man in charge of the wedding feast didn't know where all the wine was coming from. He told the bridegroom that he was amazed, because the wine Jesus had made was far far better than the wine that had run out.

Only Jesus' mother and his twelve chief friends realized what he was saying to them in all this. He meant them to know that what he had to say and do for his heavenly father was greater than anything anyone had ever known before, just as the new wine was better than wine that had ever been drunk before.

Jesus wanted people to understand that he came not to destroy the old ways of the children of Israel but to make them all new again. Later, one of his followers called John, who lived on an island called Patmos, was helped by God's spirit to see into the future. He saw, he said, "a new heaven and a new earth." And there was Jesus, making everything new and glorious.

This was what Jesus had said when he was on earth. Peter once asked him what would happen to all those who had given up many things to follow Jesus. Jesus said that everything would be made new and they would be rewarded with a hundred times more than everything they had given up or had had before..

This is what he started to show them when he turned the water into wine at Cana.

Matthew 19, 28–29; John 2, 1–12; Revelation 1, 9; 21, 1–8.

Jesus Feeds Many People

Just as Jesus could produce wine at a wedding, so if he wished he could feed people in a way that taught them new things. Once a very large crowd followed him because of all the people he had healed. He climbed up a hillside and sat down.

Then he looked up and saw the great crowd approaching. To one of his friends, called Philip, he said, "Can we buy some food to feed them?" He was testing Philip, to see if he believed that Jesus could do anything. Philip said, "We haven't enough money to buy even a small piece of food for each one of these people."

Then Andrew, Peter's brother, came up with a small boy who had five loaves made of barley and two small fishes. Jesus said, "Make everyone sit down." There may have been five thousand people there.

Then Jesus took the five loaves, thanked God for them, and gave them out to everyone. He did the same with the fishes. Everybody ate some. And the disciples still collected five baskets full of the scraps that were left.

Some of the people there were so amazed that they said Jesus was like Moses, who long ago had arranged for God to feed the children of Israel with manna in the wilderness.

It was near to the feast of the Passover, so they also remembered that Moses had told them always to have a special meal at that time.

And some of the crowd even wanted to force Jesus to be their king. But Jesus went away by himself and escaped into the hills.

Matthew 14, 13–21; 15, 32–39; Mark 6, 30–44; Luke 9, 10–17; John 6, 1–15.

Jesus and Peter Walk on Water

The children of Israel used to sing a song to God praising him every time they escaped from their enemies. This song, they thought, was perhaps written by King David himself.

Their enemies were so many, they sang, that they were like great sea waves. But for the help of God, these waves would have drowned them all. God had saved them from drowning.

Jesus once taught his people that they could rely on him the way they had always relied on God. But at first only his twelve best friends saw it.

It happened while he was alone in the hills. His twelve helpers set sail on the nearby lake, so that the great crowd he had fed would go away.

Jesus that evening saw their boat far out of the water. A great wind was blowing up large waves around the boat.

Between three o'clock and six o'clock in the morning, Jesus decided to walk out across the water to them.

When they saw him walking on the water towards them, his friends were scared out of their wits. "It's a ghost," they thought. But Jesus called out to them not to be afraid.

Peter was braver than the rest. "If it's really you," he said, "tell me to come out to you, and I will." Jesus answered, "Come to me." Peter climbed out of the boat and started walking towards Jesus. But suddenly he was afraid again. The great wind was blowing him over. He began to sink.

"Save me," he cried. Jesus put his hand out and held him safe. "Why don't you really believe in me?" he asked.

Jesus and Peter got back into the boat. The wind dropped right away. The friends of Jesus remembered that God controls the winds and the sea. They bowed before him and said, "You must certainly be the son of God."

Psalm 124; Matthew 14, 22–33; Mark 6, 45–52;
John 6, 16–21.

Jesus Calms a Storm at Sea

Whenever Jesus was on a boat out at sea, he was never afraid. His friends often were – even those who had been fishermen.

One evening, Jesus and his twelve disciples were crossing a lake in a boat. Jesus was very tired. He settled down in the boat and put his head on a cushion. Soon he was fast asleep.

Suddenly, a great gale blew up. The wind blew strongly. Huge waves beat against the boat. Then water began to pour in. The men were terrified, because they thought they would all drown. But Jesus went on sleeping.

His friends were so frightened that they woke him up. "Don't you care about us?" they cried. "We're sinking."

Jesus opened his eyes and said to them, "Why are you so terrified? Don't you believe in me yet?" Then he stood up in the boat, with the waves raging all around. He spoke to the wind and the sea as if he were calming some wild animal. He

said, "Quiet down!" And they did.

Jesus's friends were again astonished. They asked themselves what kind of a man their master was. Even the wind and the sea obeyed him.

The answer to their question was in the old songs of the children of Israel. One song praised God because he could calm the mighty ocean and its great waves.

Another of their songs thanked God for his goodness to everyone in trouble, including sailors in storms. God could speak and bring about a great gale. The ships rocked about. The sailors called out to God, and he made the storm as calm as a whisper.

Now they saw that Jesus, too, had these powers. They were learning to trust him even in times of very great trouble.

Psalm 65, 7; 107, 23–30; Matthew 8, 23–27; Mark 4, 35–41; Luke 8, 22–25.

Jesus Gives New Life to Lazarus

When Jesus came to a town to talk and help people, he nearly always had friends to give him shelter and food. In the town of Bethany he would stay with a good friend called Lazarus and his two sisters, Mary and Martha.

One day, Jesus was told that Lazarus was very ill. Jesus loved Lazarus. But he decided to let him die, so as to show everyone the most marvelous thing God could do. Instead of rushing immediately to Bethany to make his friend better, Jesus stayed away for two more days. Then he set out for Bethany, which was still some days' journey away. By the time he reached there, Lazarus had been buried for four days.

Many people had come to tell Mary and Martha how sorry they were. When Jesus arrived, Mary stayed in their house, but Martha came out to greet him. She said, "If you had been here earlier, Lazarus would not have died. Even now if you asked God to help us, he would do anything for you."

Jesus asked her if she believed in the resurrection – that is, that God could bring the dead to life again. Martha said she did believe that one day God would do this. "Your brother," said Jesus, "will rise again."

Then Jesus told her that anyone who really believed in him would live again after they had died. "I am the resurrection," he said. "I am life."

Martha said, "I believe you are the son of the living God."

Then Martha sent for Mary. Mary was crying. She fell at the feet of Jesus and said she wished he had been there earlier, to stop her brother dying. When Jesus saw Mary crying, he too cried. And then they went to Lazarus's tomb.

The tomb was a cave blocked up with a great stone. Jesus made them take it away. Then he prayed to God to show his power and also to teach the people watching that he had been sent by God.

When he had prayed, Jesus said, "Lazarus, come out!"

Lazarus did so. His hands and feet were wrapped in bandages and there was a cloth around his face. Jesus said, "Take them off so that Lazarus can walk again."

John 11, 1–44.

Jesus Teaches Mary and Martha

Once when Jesus was staying with Mary and Martha, Martha seemed to be doing all the work. She was cooking the food, making sure it was properly served and seeing that everyone had all they needed.

Her sister Mary seemed to be doing nothing. She was sitting at Jesus's feet, listening carefully to all he had to say.

At last, Martha could stand this no longer. The serving was getting her down and she was tired. She came up to Jesus and said, "Tell Mary to help me. Don't you care if she leaves everything to me and does nothing herself?"

Jesus answered, "Martha, stop fussing about everything. You worry too much. Really, all you should care about are my words. Mary has chosen to listen to them. No one must take that away from her."

Luke 10, 38–42.

Jesus Loves Children

Jesus especially loved children and they loved him. Mothers would often bring babies for him to bless. The friends of Jesus once tried to stop them from doing this. They thought the mothers were wasting Jesus' time. But Jesus was very angry. He said, "Let little children come to me. Don't try to stop them." He put his arms around the children, put his hand on their heads and blessed them.

He loved children because they didn't behave as if they were the greatest persons in the world. They were too little and weak.

Once, when his best friends were arguing about which of them was the greatest, he took a little child, set him by his side and said, "If you look after a child because I have told you to, you are caring for me and for God who sent me."

Jesus believed that the least person should be looked after best. He told people that children were all members of God's kingdom, and that anyone else who wanted to get into God's kingdom must be as gentle and innocent as a little child.

Matthew 18, 1–5; *19*, 13–15; *Mark 10*, 13–16; *Luke 9*, 46–48; *19*, 15–17.

A Rich Young Man and a Woman in Trouble

Jesus didn't always manage to make people agree with him. Sometimes this was because they were too greedy to give up everything they possessed and follow him – even though they knew he was right.

Jesus told people how dangerous it was to be rich. He told a story about a rich man who had so much food from his land that he could not store it all. But he was very pleased with all these crops. He built bigger and bigger barns to hold the grain. He thought only of how rich he was. And he decided to have a good time and care about nothing else. He was very selfish. He never thought of God. But God said, "You are a fool. This very night you will die and have to face me."

People who kept everything they could get hold of found it hard to leave it all when Jesus asked them to be one of his helpers. He told them to decide which was the most important thing: money, food and treasures – or God. "Where you keep your treasure," he said, "there is your heart."

Once a rich young man came to Jesus. Jesus liked him very much. The man asked how he could lead a heavenly life. Jesus said, "Obey all the rules Moses brought from God."

The rich young man asked if he should do anything more. "Yes," said Jesus. "Sell everything you possess. Give the money you make to the poor. Then follow me and you will be perfect." But the rich young man loved his money too much. He went away, very sad, and Jesus was sad to see him go.

Although Jesus wanted people to be good, he condemned those who pretended they were good when they were not. He said, "Don't criticize other people for their wrongs, unless you want God to criticize you in the same way."

Once a woman had been caught taking someone else's husband. Those who followed the law of Moses decided to

kill her by throwing stones at her. The people who had caught her knew Jesus believed in forgiving those who were sorry for what they had done wrong. They thought they could now trap him into saying that the law of Moses about taking other people's husbands need not be obeyed. So they brought her to Jesus and said, "What should we do to her?"

Jesus knew they were out to trap him. He said, "Any person who has never done an evil thing should throw the first stone at this woman." They all realized that they could not throw the stone, for none of them was perfect. One by one they crept away. Only Jesus and the woman were left.

"Has no one condemned you?" asked Jesus. "I don't either. Now you can go away free. But don't do evil things any more."

Matthew 6, 19–21; 7, 1–5; 19, 16–22; Mark 10, 17–22; Luke 12, 33–34; 18, 18–23; John 8, 1–11.

Riding into Jerusalem

Jesus knew that people wanted to kill him and they hoped to catch him in Jerusalem. He decided to go there and show himself to everyone.

He arranged for two of his chief helpers to bring him a donkey that no one had ever ridden. Jesus had arranged a special signal with the man who owned the donkey. It was to be tied by a door in an open street. Jesus' helpers would untie it. When a man came out to ask what they were doing, they were to reply, "The master needs it. As soon as he has finished with it, we'll send the donkey back."

That was how they brought the donkey to Jesus. As a saddle, they put their own cloaks on its back. Jesus sat on the donkey and set off for Jerusalem. A great crowd gathered to see him. To show they loved Jesus, they threw their cloaks in front of the donkey, so that he could ride over them. Others cut down branches from the trees and waved them in the air, shouting, "Hurrah!"

Long ago, a prophet called Zechariah had said that the greatest king of Jerusalem would come into the city not riding on a war-horse but humbly on a don-key. The people remem-bered this. They called Jesus the son of David, and they now thought that Jesus would become a king as great as David had been. Waving their branches over Jesus they shouted, "Let us bless the one who comes in God's name."

They shouted, "Here is the one who comes in God's name." They cried, "Peace in heaven." And others shouted. "Jerusalem, your king is coming riding on a donkey."

The whole city was asking about him. The people replied, "It's the prophet Jesus, the Nazarene."

Zechariah 9, 9; Matthew 21, 1–11; Mark 11, 1–11; Luke 19, 28–38; John 12, 12–16.

Jesus Clears the Temple

As soon as Jesus reached Jerusalem, he went into the Temple. He knew that many people did not use the Temple properly. They were not interested in praying to God, but only in making money.

Some people said that the blind and the lame shouldn't go into God's temple. Jesus knew this was not right. He had healed them to show that God loved them. Now, those who couldn't see and those who couldn't walk properly came to him inside the Temple. There he cured them. This only made his enemies angrier.

They didn't like to hear the children singing that Jesus was one of the members of King David's family. But Jesus was ready for them. He asked them if they had never sung or heard of the old song of the children of Israel which said that babies in their mothers' arms would sing about the greatness of God. Now babies were singing about Jesus' greatness.

Then Jesus turned on those people who had made God's Temple into a kind of marketplace. These people sold pigeons to those who wanted to make burnt offerings to God. They also changed people's money, especially those who came to the Temple from abroad with foreign coins wanting to change them into the coins used in the Temple.

Jesus knew this was not what God's house was for. He shouted to them the words of the prophet Isaiah, "'My house,' says God, 'will be called a house of prayer for every nation.'" Jesus said, "You have made it into a home for robbers."

He made a whip out of some cord. He turned over the tables of those who changed money. He upset the seats of the people who sold doves. And he threw them all out of the Temple.

II Samuel 5, 8; Psalm 8, 2; Isaiah 56, 7; Matthew 21, 12–17; Mark 11, 11 and 15–17; Luke 19, 45–46; John 2, 14–16.

Jesus is Anointed

It was now nearly the time of the Passover. Many of Jesus' enemies thought that he ought to be killed. They said, "This man is behaving like a king. The Romans who rule us don't want us to have a king of our own. If we don't stop Jesus and put an end to him, the Roman soldiers will come and pull down our Temple. They will kill us all."

A man called Caiaphas, who was chief priest for that year, said, "It's better that one man should die to save all the rest." So they planned to kill Jesus.

Six days before the Passover, Jesus was at a party in Bethany, in the house of a man called Simon who had been a

leper. During the meal a woman came to Jesus. Often when people came into a house from the dusty street, they would wash their feet in water and put some scent on their hair. This woman had a jar of very expensive ointment. With this she washed Jesus' feet. And she poured some over his head. She then sat at his feet, wiping them with her hair.

Now one of Jesus' chief helpers was planning to go over to the side of Jesus' enemies. His name was Judas Iscariot. His job was to look after the money belonging to those who went about with Jesus. When he saw what was happening he was very angry. He didn't like anyone showing such love towards Jesus. "Why didn't this woman give the expensive ointment to us?" he asked. "We could have sold it for a lot of money and given it to the poor."

Jesus knew he was going to be killed soon. He said, "You will always be able to find poor people to give money to. But you won't always have me with you." Then Jesus said, "Just as people put beautiful scents on the bodies of dead people whom they love, so this woman has anointed my body, because you will soon have to bury me."

The man who was giving the party for Jesus was also angry. The young woman had done many evil things in her life. He wondered why Jesus was letting such a bad person wash his feet and put scent on his hair.

Jesus knew that the woman had been wicked and he also knew what the man was thinking. He turned to him and said, "When I came in, Simon, you didn't let me wash my feet. You didn't even greet me with a kiss. This woman has scented my hair and washed my feet."

He said to the woman, "I forgive you all your wrongs. What you have done for me will be remembered throughout the world, whenever people talk of God's good news."

Matthew 26, 6–12; Mark 14, 3–9; Luke 7, 36–50; John 11, 45–54; 12, 1–9.

Trick Questions

The enemies of Jesus now started to try to trick him in every possible way. They wanted to make him say things that would get him into trouble. Then they could either have him put into prison or, they hoped, killed.

But Jesus was always too clever for them. He said to them, "You don't like whatever anyone does who has been sent by God. John the Baptist came to earth and decided to eat almost no food and drink almost no drink. You said, 'He's mad.' Now I come doing different things from John. I love being at parties with my friends, but you say, 'He's always eating and drinking too much.' You're like silly children who don't know what games to play. They can't decide whether to dance in the streets or cry by the roadside."

Once Jesus' enemies found his friends picking grain on the seventh day of the week and eating it. They came to Jesus. "Look," they said, "your friends work on the seventh day, when God told us to rest." Jesus knew that they were trying to get him into trouble, by making him say that God's rules didn't need to be obeyed. He said, "I'm in charge of what happens on the seventh day of the week."

To show them that he didn't care about their criticisms, he went straight to the Temple and healed a man whose arm was withered. Because it was the seventh day, his enemies became very angry indeed and wanted to get rid of him.

Their plan was to try to get him in trouble first with the leading Jews and then with the Romans who at that time

ruled all of them. To get him in trouble with the Jews, Jesus' enemies said that he had told his friends not to pay money to keep the Temple standing and pay for its services. But they were wrong. Jesus said he didn't need to pay. He could always decide not to. But even so, he did give money to the Temple, so his enemies couldn't attack him for not doing so.

To get him in trouble with the Romans his enemies asked him whether or not money should be paid to them as well. Some people didn't like paying this money to people who had captured their land. So Jesus would be disliked by these people if he said "Pay money to the Romans." If he said, "Don't pay," he would be in trouble with the Romans.

This was a very tricky question, and his enemies tried to make him give a foolish answer by pretending to praise him. They said, "We know you always speak the truth. You don't care what people think of you. It makes no difference to you whether the person you are talking to is important. All you care about is what God wants. So answer our question."

Jesus saw that they did not mean the nice things they were saying about him. "Why are you trying to trick me?" he asked. Then he said, "Show me a Roman coin." When they brought one, he said, "There is a name and a picture of a man's head on this coin. Whom do they belong to?" They answered, "To Caesar, the ruler of all the Romans." Then Jesus said, "You must give to Caesar what belongs to him. But you must also give to God what belongs to God."

Yet in spite of all Jesus' cleverness, they hated him more and more. They didn't like to hear the truth from him. For instance, he knew that one day the Temple in Jerusalem would be pulled down again. "Not a stone of it will remain," he said. His enemies hated to hear that most of all.

Matthew 11, 16–19; 12, 1–14; 17, 24–27; 22, 23–33; 24, 1–2; Mark 12, 13–17; 13, 1–2; Luke 6, 1–11; 7, 31–35; 20, 20–26; 21, 5–6.

Jesus' Last Supper

Since he knew he was going to be killed, Jesus thought it was time to tell his friends how they should remember him after his death.

He did this at the feast of the Passover. He decided that he and his friends should eat this special meal together, and then ever afterwards his friends could remember him by having such a meal together. So secretly, taking great care that no one should find out where they were, he arranged for himself and his best friends to meet in a room high up in a house in Jerusalem. His friends were to find the room by following a man, whom they should recognize because he would be carrying a jar of water.

But Judas Iscariot was among these friends. By now he was ready to tell Jesus' enemies where he was. Jesus knew this. At the meal, he told everyone that one of those sitting at the table would hand him over to his enemies. They all said, "It can't be me." And they were all saddened.

At the meal Jesus told his friends many things that he had until then kept from them. He said that soon he would be leaving them; but very soon after that he would be with them again. He said, "Don't be surprised if a lot of people hate you. That is because they love the things of this world, not the things of God. And remember, they had no reason to hate me, but they did."

Then, while they were all eating, Jesus took some bread. He thanked God for it. He broke it and said, "Take and eat this. It is my body. I am going to give my body for you." Then he gave it to them. Next he took some wine. He thanked God for that. He said, "Every one of you must drink some of this. It is my blood, which is to be poured out for you."

Jesus told them to do this to remember him. He said he would not again drink wine until he did so with his heavenly father.

Matthew 26, 17–19 and 26–29; Mark 14, 12–16 and 22–25; Luke 22, 2–13 and 15–20; John 15, 18; 16, 16.

The Garden of Gethsemane

Jesus did not want to be killed. In those days, killing included beating and then slow pain. He prayed that God would not let him suffer long.

After the last supper with his friends, Jesus went to a mountain of olive trees near Jerusalem. At the bottom of this mountain was a garden called Gethsemane, which means 'oil-press'. His friends Peter, James and John went with him.

Jesus said, "I am very sad." Even though it was late, he asked his three friends not to go to sleep. "Stay here with me," he said, "and keep awake."

Then he went a little farther on. There he knelt down to pray. First, he prayed that God would not let him be hurt in the way his enemies planned. He was so sad while he prayed that he began to sweat; and his sweat fell to the ground like huge drops of blood.

After he had prayed he came back to Peter, James and John. They were asleep. "Couldn't you stay awake with me?" he asked Peter. "You should pray that you will not be in trouble the way I am in trouble." Then he went away from them a second time to pray to God.

This time his prayer was different. He said, "Father, if I have to be hurt in this way, then I will do what you wish."

Again he came back to his friends, Peter, James and John. For a second time they had gone to sleep. This time Jesus didn't wake them up. He went away from them again, once more to tell his heavenly father that he was willing to die. Then he came back to his sleeping friends and said, "You can carry on sleeping now. There's nothing more to do."

But a moment later the enemies of Jesus came to arrest him. So he said to his helpers, "Wake up. The man who plans to give me over to my enemies is near."

Matthew 26, 26–46; Mark 14, 26 and 32–42; Luke 22, 39–46.

Jesus is Arrested

Judas Iscariot was leading the group of soldiers and the servants of the chief priest who came to arrest Jesus in the Garden of Gethsemane. The soldiers carried swords and clubs. Because it was dark, others carried lamps and torches.

None of them knew Jesus well enough to recognize him. But Judas Iscariot had arranged a special signal with the soldier. He would go up to Jesus and identify him by kissing him. That is what he did. Jesus saw him and said, "My friend, do what you have to do." Judas kissed him. Jesus said, "Do you show me to my enemies by kissing me?"

Then the soldiers rushed forward. Peter wanted to fight to save Jesus. He took out his sword, and with it he chopped off the right ear of one of those who had come to take Jesus away. This man was a servant of the chief priest and was called Malchus. But Jesus said to Peter, "Put your sword back in its sheath. Anyone who lives by fighting will die by fighting." Jesus said that if he had wished, he could have asked God to save him. God would have sent many of his messengers to protect Jesus from the soldiers.

To show that he didn't want to hurt those who were coming to seize him, Jesus touched the right ear of the servant of the chief priest, and it was better again.

At first, those who had come to seize him couldn't do so. When they saw Jesus, they all fell back. But Jesus said, "Am I a robber, that you have come for me with these swords and clubs? For many days I was sitting in the Temple teaching people. You could easily have taken me then." Then he said, "Since you are looking only for me, let these other men go."

So the soldiers took Jesus away. And all his friends ran off.

Matthew 26, 47–56; Mark 14, 43–50; Luke 22, 47–53; John 18, 3–11.

Jesus is Sentenced to Death

At first Jesus was taken to the house of Caiaphas who was the chief priest. With Caiaphas were the other members of the court. They tried to make Jesus say something against God. But they could not. Then they brought in several people to tell lies about Jesus. But because these people were liars, they said different things about Jesus. They could not agree among themselves. This made the chief priest and his friends look silly.

So next they decided to question Jesus about all he had said and done. Jesus asked why they were doing this now. Anyone could have come to hear him when he was teaching and talking to people in the open. He never hid anything. They could have found out everything about him then.

For most of the time Jesus said nothing. They asked him all sorts of questions and said bad things about him. He wouldn't speak to them, but when they asked, "Are you the specially chosen servant and son of God?" he answered, "I am and you will see that it is so."

The chief priest then stood up. To show how angry he was, he tore his own clothing. He said to everyone else, "We do not need witnesses now, he has insulted our God. This man claims *he* is God." That, the chief priest thought, was a very evil thing to do. "What should we do with him?" he asked. They answered, "Now he must die."

Then they started spitting at Jesus. They put a blindfold on him and beat him with their fists. They said, "Be a prophet, specially chosen one of God. Tell us which one of us hit you." They made fun of Jesus.

Peter's Denial

Now Peter was in the courtyard of the chief priest's house, looking through the open door. He could see Jesus inside. He could see people mocking him by spitting at him and hitting him with their fists.

He was very scared, in case he'd be caught too and perhaps also beaten and killed. But he didn't want to leave Jesus, because he had promised never to let him down. Jesus had sadly told him, "Before the cock crows in the morning, you'll pretend three times that you never knew me."

It was very cold, nearly morning, and a fire was burning in the courtyard. Peter was sitting by the fire, warming himself. Suddenly a servant of the chief priest pointed at him. "You were with Jesus, weren't you?" she said. Peter was frightened. "I don't know what you're talking about," he lied, and ran to hide in the shadow of the gateway.

But another servant saw him. She was related to the man whose ear Peter had cut off, so she had good reason to remember him. "Didn't I see you in the olive garden with Jesus?" she said. "No!" cried Peter. "I don't know him."

Soon everybody was crowding around him. "Of course you were with Jesus," they said. "You come from the same place as he does. We can tell by the way you talk." To try to stop them saying these things, Peter began to say the most hateful words against Jesus.

At that moment he heard a cock crowing because it was morning. Peter remembered what Jesus had said to him, and he began to cry.

Pontius Pilate

The elders who had been questioning Jesus decided to take him to Pontius Pilate, the man who governed them on behalf of Caesar. The chief priest and the other enemies of Jesus said he had been telling everyone to rise up and fight against the Romans. They said Jesus told people not to pay money to the Romans. They said Jesus was saying he was king of the Jews.

Pontius Pilate asked Jesus if he did claim to be king. Jesus answered, "I have a kingdom, but it is not in this world. All I wish to do here is tell people the truth." Pilate asked "What is the truth?" But he believed Jesus was not as bad as Jesus's enemies said. Pontius Pilate thought the best thing to do was to have Jesus beaten and then let him go.

Pilate tried to get out of judging Jesus. Since Jesus was from Galilee, he sent him there to be tried by the man who ruled Galilee at the time. This man was called Herod and happened to be in Jerusalem. But Jesus would say nothing to Herod. So Herod got his guards to make fun of Jesus, while Herod watched and joined in. They pretended to dress him as a king. Then they sent him back to Pontius Pilate.

Pontius Pilate still wanted to set Jesus free, and he had an idea for doing this. Every year, at the time of the feast of the Passover, Pilate used to set free a prisoner, hoping this would please the Jews. He decided to ask the crowd outside whether he should set Jesus free, or a rebel called Barabbas who stole from people and killed them. He knew that Jesus' enemies had brought Jesus to him because they were jealous. So Pontius Pilate took Jesus out to the crowd and asked, "Shall I set free Jesus or shall I set free Barabbas?"

"Crucify Him, Crucify Him!"

Jesus' enemies ruined Pontius Pilate's plan to set Jesus free. They went among the crowd and made everyone shout, "Set Barabbas free." Pilate asked the crowd, "What shall I do

with Jesus?" Jesus' enemies wanted Jesus killed by nailing him to a cross until he died. This was called "crucifixion". They mingled with the crowd and shouted "Crucify him!"

Pontius Pilate did not like this. He knew Jesus was a good man. He took a bowl of water and washed his hands in front of the crowd. He wanted to show that he wasn't the one who was having Jesus killed. His hands were clean. The crowd shouted, "We'll take the blame for killing Jesus." And so Pontius Pilate gave the order that Jesus was to be crucified.

Matthew 26, 57–75; 27, 1–26; Mark 14, 53–72; 15, 1–15; Luke 22, 54–71; 23, 1–25; John 18, 12–40.

Mocking Jesus

Those who hated Jesus were very cruel to him. People said he was king of the Jews, but now he was going to be killed. The soldiers of Pilate took him away. Then they took off all his clothes and dressed him in the cloak of a king.

Kings used to carry a rod in their hands. The soldiers beat Jesus on the head with a rod before putting it into his hand.

Kings wore crowns on their heads. The soldiers made a crown for Jesus; but it was a crown twisted out of twigs filled with thorns. They pushed it onto his head.

They spat at him and beat him. And then they made fun by bowing down before him and saying, "We are your servants, king of the Jews."

Pontius Pilate didn't like this. He went out once again to the crowd and shouted to them, "Watch. I'm going to bring to you the man who has done nothing wrong, so far as I can see." Then he brought Jesus out to them, in the cloak of a king and with the crown of thorns on his head. "Look at the man," said Pontius Pilate. But the crowd, led by Jesus' enemies, shouted louder and louder, "Crucify him!"

Pontius Pilate was now very frightened. He said to Jesus, "I want to know where you come from." When Jesus wouldn't speak to him, Pontius Pilate said, "You know I can do anything to you." Jesus replied, "You can't do anything unless my heavenly father gives you power to do it."

The crowd outside was shouting more and more, and Pontius Pilate gave in. Jesus was led off to be crucified. He was so tired by now that he could not carry the cross on which he was to be nailed. The soldiers found a man called Simon, who had come to Jerusalem from Cyrene where he lived, and made him follow Jesus, carrying the cross.

Matthew 27, 27–32; Mark 15, 16–22; Luke 23, 26–32; John 19, 1–17.

Jesus on the Cross

At Golgotha, outside Jerusalem, the soldiers guarding Jesus took off his clothes. Usually the soldiers divided the clothes of people they crucified among themselves. Jesus was wearing a cloak that was all of one piece. Instead of cutting it up, the soldiers played a game and the winner took Jesus' cloak.

They nailed Jesus to the cross through his hands and his feet and raised it up high and stuck it into the ground.

On the cross was written, "Jesus of Nazareth, king of the Jews." Pontius Pilate had written this. Jesus' enemies wanted him to change what he had written to "This man said he was king of the Jews." But Pontius Pilate wouldn't.

On either side of Jesus two robbers were crucified. Some of the people watching now made fun of him. "He used to help other people," they laughed, "but he can't help himself now." Even one of the crucified robbers made fun of him. But the other stopped him. "Jesus has done nothing wrong," he said. Then this robber asked Jesus to help him when he died. Jesus said, "We'll be in heaven together this day."

Jesus began to sing to himself one of the old songs of the Jews – the one beginning, "My God, my God, why have you left me all alone?" Near the cross stood Mary his mother, his mother's sister, and some of his other friends. He looked down at his mother. He told her that one of the men standing by would now look after her as if he were her own son.

Then Jesus said, "I'm thirsty," and a soldier held up a sponge which had been dipped in sour wine on the end of a spear. Jesus was now nearly dead. He said, "It is all finished. Father I put my life into your hands." And then Jesus died. The chief of his guards had seen everything that had happened and said, "This must have been the son of God."

Psalm 22; Matthew 27, 32–56; Mark 15, 21–41; Luke 23, 26–49; John 19, 17–37.

Jesus is Buried and is Alive Again

To make sure that Jesus was dead, a soldier pushed a spear into his side. Then one of Jesus' secret followers, a man called Joseph of Arimathea, asked Pontius Pilate if he could put Jesus' body in his own tomb. Pilate agreed. Jesus's body was taken down from the cross. It was placed into this tomb, which was new, and a great stone put over the entrance.

The following day was the seventh day of the week, so the women who were to put scents on his body rested. Very early on Sunday morning they came back to the tomb. But they couldn't find Jesus anywhere inside it. The stone had been rolled away. Inside were messengers of God, who told the women that Jesus was not there. He was alive again. If they went to Galilee, they said, there they would meet him.

The women were Mary Magdalene, Mary the mother of James, and Salome, the wife of Zebedee. A messenger of God

at the tomb told them to go and tell Jesus' friends and helpers that he was alive. But the women were too scared to.

Mary Magdalene stayed by the tomb, crying. She saw Peter and another follower of Jesus whom Jesus had loved very much. She said to them, "Someone has taken Jesus' body out of the tomb. I don't know where they have put it." So both the men ran to the tomb. Peter got there last, but Jesus' other friend didn't go inside first. Peter led him in, and they both saw the clothes that had wrapped Jesus's body lying there empty. They both knew he must be alive again.

Mary Magdalene was still crying outside. She saw through her tears a man standing there. "It must be the gardener," she thought. But it was Jesus. Only when he called her name did she recognize his voice. And then she was very happy.

Matthew 27, 56–66; 28, 1–8; Mark 15, 42–47; 16, 1–8; Luke 23, 50–56; 24, 1–8; John 19, 38–42; 20, 1–18.

Jesus Returns

After this, more people saw Jesus alive. Most were frightened because they had never known anything like it before.

On a Sunday his best friends were hiding in a room because they were scared that Jesus' enemies might catch them. Suddenly Jesus was with them. He said, "Be at peace." They were truly happy then. He showed them where the nails of the cross had gone into his hands and feet, and where the spear had gone into his side.

One of his friends, Thomas the twin, was not there at the time. When the other friends of Jesus told Thomas what they had seen, he did not believe them. He said, "I need to put my fingers into the holes where the nails went and my hand into the hole made in Jesus' side by the soldier's spear. Only when I've done that will I believe."

The following Sunday they were all together again. This time Thomas was there too. Jesus was suddenly with them. He let Thomas feel the holes in his hands and side. Thomas said, "You are my God. You are the one I obey."

At another time Peter, Thomas the twin, James and John, and three more of Jesus' chief helpers went fishing. They were out all night and caught nothing. Then a man appeared on the shore, and shouted, "Throw your net over the other side of the boat." They did and caught lots of fish. Then Peter and the others knew that the man on the shore was Jesus.

When they reached the shore, Jesus was there cooking breakfast for them. They ate bread, and fish cooked on a charcoal fire. After the meal Jesus three times asked Peter whether he loved him. Peter was upset at being asked so many times. "You know I love you," he replied. But Jesus needed to be sure that Peter would look after the first people who followed Jesus now he was risen from death. He said to Peter, "Feed my sheep." And he also said, "Follow me."

Jesus appeared to his friends at other times. Two of his

friends were one day walking towards a village called Emmaus, which was a little way from Jerusalem. They were talking about everything that had happened. As yet they did not know about Jesus being alive. Jesus came up to them and walked by their side, but he did not let them see who he was. He said, "Why are you so sad?" They answered, "Everyone in Jerusalem knows why. We hoped that Jesus of Nazareth would set us all free and rule over us as a new king of the Jews."

Jesus said, "You don't understand." And he explained how all the prophets had suffered and explained how being hurt could do good things, if it helped other people. Jesus explained that God himself had wanted Jesus to die on the cross. The two men were made happy and excited by hearing this. They asked Jesus to stay for a meal with them. He agreed. And as he broke the bread, they realized who he was. Then he vanished.

Luke 24, 13–43; John 20, 19–29; 21, 1–29.

213

Jesus Joins His Heavenly Father

In Galilee the eleven main followers of Jesus (all, that is, except Judas Iscariot) met together. Jesus had told them to meet him there. They saw him and all fell down before him – though some of them were still not sure that it could be Jesus they were seeing. How could he be alive when he had died?

Jesus said, "Now I rule over all heaven and earth. You must go to the people of every land. Tell them about me. Teach them to follow me. And baptize them." He said, "Until the end of all time, I shall be with you."

Then they went to Bethany. He blessed them, and there he left them, disappearing into a cloud.

Now they were very happy that Jesus was alive. They went back to Jerusalem, praising God and worshiping him in the temple.

Matthew 28, 16–20; Luke 24, 44–53; Acts 1, 6–11.

The Young Church

The first people who followed Jesus after he had risen from death did all that he had told them.

They prayed. They remembered his orders that they should have special meals, so each week they met together to break bread, as he had done, to thank God for it and to share it out. They remembered he had said, "This is my body." At the same time they poured out wine, to be shared by everyone once they had thanked God for it too. They remembered Jesus's words, "This is my blood."

Because Jesus had told them how much God disliked evil greedy people, and because he had taught them to love and care for the poor, they decided it would be best if they shared every possession. Nobody said of anything, "This is mine." Everything belonged to the whole group.

Judas, when he realized what an evil thing he had done in giving Jesus to his enemies, had killed himself. He was paid thirty pieces of silver for taking the soldiers to Jesus. He had been filled with sadness and tried to give the money back. But those wicked men who had paid him wouldn't take it. Judas flung the money at their feet, went out and hung himself.

In the place of Judas, the eleven faithful followers of Jesus chose a man called Matthias, who had known Jesus from the time John the Baptist started preaching in the desert. Now they were twelve again.

They all waited until Jesus would keep his promise that the spirit of God would come into them.

Matthew 27, 3–10; Acts 1, 15–26; 2, 42–47.

The First Pentecost Sunday

All the followers of Jesus met together to remember all he had done, forty days after he had joined his heavenly father. With them was Jesus' mother, Mary, some of his relatives and other women who had been his friends. They were all together in one room.

Suddenly, there was a terrifying sound. It was as if a great wind was filling the room. It came from heaven, and they knew it was caused by the spirit of God. And then flames appeared in the room. These flames divided themselves among everyone in the room. No one was burned because these flames came from God, just as the seraph had placed a burning coal on Isaiah's lips without burning him.

Now, like Isaiah, the people began to speak for God. God's spirit made them speak in foreign languages that they had never spoken before. Knowing that God's spirit was blessing

them, they went outside to speak to the people of Jerusalem.

Jerusalem was a holy city of God, and those who loved God came there from all over the world. There were people of many nations and religions. Jesus had ordered his friends to tell every nation in the world about him. These visitors to Jerusalem, who spoke many different languages, were surprised to hear Jesus' friends talking to them in their own languages. It didn't matter where the people came from for they could all hear about how wonderful God was and understand it.

But some people laughed because the friends of Jesus were making all this noise and seemed to be so happy. They thought they had been drinking too much wine.

Peter decided he had better say something to explain what had happened. "We haven't had too much to drink," he said. "What has happened is something that a prophet called Joel once spoke about. Joel said, 'God wants his spirit to be poured on everyone. Men and women, the old and the young, sons and daughters, slaves and servants, all of them will have God's own spirit in them.'"

Then Peter told them about Jesus. He told them about the healings and other good things Jesus had done. He told them it was with God's knowledge that Jesus had been killed. Then he told them how God had given Jesus new life.

Peter remembered an old Jewish song. In it they sang of how God cried to another great one, "Sit at my right hand." And this, said Peter, is what had happened to Jesus.

Many of those listening then asked Peter how they could become Christians – as the followers of Jesus were to become known. "Be sorry for all you have done wrong," replied Peter. "Be baptized. God's spirit will come to you." That day three thousand people began to follow Jesus.

Psalm 110, 1; Isaiah 6, 6–7; Joel 3, 1–5; Acts 1, 12–14; 2, 1–41.

Ananias and Sapphira

All the early Christians shared everything they possessed and nobody was short of food or clothes. Everything was brought to the leaders, who were the ones Jesus had shown himself to after he had risen from the dead. These leaders gave out food and goods to those who needed them.

Anyone who had some land or a house for sale didn't keep the profit. They brought it to the leaders.

But a few people were still greedy. A man called Ananias and his wife Sapphira had some land to sell. They secretly agreed with each other not to give all the money they gained from selling it. They would give only part of the profit to the Christian leaders and keep the rest for themselves.

But Peter found out. He told Ananias that he could have done anything he liked with his land and with the money he made from selling it. But it was very evil to try to trick the

Christian leaders into thinking that he had given it all up. "You didn't lie to us," said Peter. "You lied to God."

Ananias was so upset about this that he fell down dead. Peter's young helpers took his body, wrapped it in a sheet and buried it. Three hours later Sapphira came in. She didn't know what had happened to her husband.

Peter asked Sapphira, "How much did you get when you sold your land?" She didn't tell him the truth. Then he said, "I see that you and Ananias both agreed to try to trick God."

"Do you hear those footsteps?" he went on. "They are those of my young helpers who have just buried your husband. The same thing will happen to you." At this Sapphira too fell down dead.

Many people learned from this that it is a very dangerous thing to try to trick God or lie to him.

Acts 4, 32–36; 5, 1–11.

Stephen is Stoned to Death

After Jesus was crucified, his enemies became the enemies of his followers who were now called Christians. After the death of Jesus, one man who had not been a Christian for long – a man called Stephen – was the first to suffer death at the hands of these enemies.

Stephen could do wonderful things, because God's spirit was with him. He used to argue with those who would not follow Jesus, trying to show how wrong they were.

Stephen's enemies began to tell lies about him. They said he was rude about the Temple in Jerusalem. They said he didn't obey the rules of God given by Moses. Stephen was arrested and brought to trial before the chief priest.

The chief priest asked Stephen if the things said against him were true. Stephen then made a speech. In it he showed how the children of Israel had sometimes turned against God's prophets and messengers. For example they turned against Moses and made a golden calf, forgetting all the good things Moses had done for them because of God. They were given God's rules and then sometimes failed to obey them.

Stephen told the people that God had planned to show himself perfectly to his people. He had done this by sending Jesus to them. Prophets had longed to see God's specially chosen servant. Sometimes the children of Israel had killed those prophets. And now, in killing Jesus, they had killed God's specially chosen one too.

This was too much for the enemies of Stephen. His words made them very angry indeed. They were being blamed for killing God's son who had done nothing wrong.

Then Stephen made them even angrier. He said he could see into heaven, where Jesus had the highest place next to God.

They didn't want to hear this. They put their hands over their ears to try to keep out Stephen's words. They shouted at him. And finally they seized him and carried him outside the walls of the city.

There they threw great stones at him until he was dead. As they were doing this, Stephen said, "Jesus my God, take my life into your hands." Then he knelt down and said, "Forgive them, Jesus, for what they are doing." And so he died.

Acts 6, 8–15; Acts 7.

Saul Changes his Name

There was a man called Saul who disliked Christians so much that he wanted to kill them all. He used to take them to court, hoping they would be sentenced to death. He would also help other people to kill them. When people were throwing stones at Stephen to kill him, they took off their coats so as to throw better, and Saul took care of their coats for them.

But then he began to wonder if the Christians were right after all. Maybe their master Jesus was the son of God. Saul tried to push these thoughts out of his mind. He went to the chief priest in the Temple and asked if he could arrest as many followers of Jesus he could find and bring them to Jerusalem.

Saul set out on the road to Damascus, to try to catch some Christians there. About midday he was almost at the city when a blinding light flashed all around him. He fell to the ground, terrified. Then he heard a voice saying, "Saul, Saul, why do you keep attacking me?" "Who are you?" asked the frightened Saul. "I am Jesus," was the reply, "and you keep attacking me."

The men who were with Saul didn't know what to say. Some of them could hear the voice, but they couldn't see anybody. "What shall I do?" asked Saul. "Stand up," answered Jesus. "I want you to work for me all over the world. When you get to Damascus, there you will find out what to do."

Saul stood up and opened his eyes, but he couldn't see anything. The men had to hold his hands and lead him into Damascus. For three days he didn't eat or drink.

Then a man called Ananias came to see him. Ananias was a follower of Jesus. He had heard the voice of Jesus telling him to go and see Saul. Ananias didn't want to do this at all. "Lord," he said, "many people have told me that this man hates your followers and tries to hurt them whenever he can. Why do you want me to go and see him?"

But Jesus said that Saul was now going to work with the Christians all over the world. He was going to speak for Jesus to everyone. Ananias, no longer afraid, went to see Saul and blessed him. He said, "Brother Saul, see again." Instantly Saul could see.

Saul was baptized there and then, and he took some food for the first time in three days. A few days later he went to where the Jews worshiped. Everyone was amazed. What had happened to Saul? The man who once hated all Christians was now saying, "Jesus is the son of God." To show everyone that he had completely changed, Saul changed his name to Paul.

Acts 9, 1–22. Acts 22, 3–21. Acts 26, 9–23. Galatians 1, 11–17.

Paul Escapes from Damascus

Now that Paul had become a Christian, he was attacked by those who had once been on his side. They were now his enemies.

He was a very good speaker. When he went into a temple at Damascus, saying that Jesus is the son of God, people were amazed. "Isn't this the man who spent all his time trying to put the Christians into prison? Didn't he come here to arrest many of them?" they asked. But now Paul was always thinking of ways to show that his new beliefs were right.

So some of them decided to kill him. They hoped to catch him the moment he left the city of Damascus. They kept watch on all the gates, but Paul was much too clever for them. As soon as he heard what they were planning, he got his new Christian friends to lower him in a strong basket from the top of one of the city walls after dark.

So he escaped. But for the rest of his life people continued to try to get him into trouble. He was often sent to prison. On five different occasions his enemies lashed him. Three times he was beaten with a stick. Once great stones were thrown at him by those who hated him, but they didn't kill him.

Because he traveled everywhere, telling people about Jesus, he lived a dangerous life. Sometimes he had no food or drink and nearly starved to death. He sometimes had to sleep in the open air. In the countryside robbers attacked him. At sea he was three times in danger when the ships he was in began to sink. After one shipwreck he spent a day and night floating in the water.

But Paul endured all this because he wanted to tell the whole world about his master Jesus.

Acts 9, 20–25; II Corinthians 11, 21–33.

Peter's Strange Dream

Paul traveled the world telling people about Jesus. Until then all Christians had been Jews. But soon many people who were not Jews were hearing about Jesus. Some of them wanted to join his friends.

The Jews had many rules about food which those people who were not Jews did not follow. For instance, Jews did not eat camels. They didn't eat pigs and they didn't eat hares. There were some sea animals they didn't eat, as well as some birds. The creatures they didn't eat they called 'unclean'. But other people – Romans, Greeks and so on – did not mind eating these animals.

The question now arose whether those people who weren't Jews but who wanted to become Christians should stop eating these 'unclean' beasts?

One of them was a Roman soldier called Cornelius. He was an officer. He lived in Jerusalem and very much respected

Jews and was respected by them. He and his whole family loved God and tried to obey him. They gave money to people who needed it. Each day they prayed to God.

God decided that Cornelius and his family should become Christians. One day Cornelius saw God's messenger come into his house. The messenger told him that his life had pleased God.

He told Cornelius to send servants to a place called Jaffa, where they would find Peter. They should bring Peter to Cornelius's house. Then the messenger of God vanished.

Cornelius did as he had been told. He sent three of his servants and one of his soldiers to find Peter.

While they were on their way, Peter was at prayer. It was just before dinner-time and he was hungry. He suddenly had a dream. In this dream he saw a great sheet let down from heaven. In this sheet were all sorts of 'unclean' beasts. Then Peter heard the voice of God telling him, "Kill one of these beasts and eat it."

Peter said, "I will not. I have never eaten an unclean animal in all my life." But in the dream God said, "I made all these animals. Nothing made by me which can be eaten is unclean." God repeated this three times, so that Peter could make no mistake about what he was saying.

Peter learned a lot from this dream. He learned that those who lived in different ways from the way he lived were not for that reason bad. He learned that people could become Christians without changing their eating habits, and without taking up the food-rules of the Jews.

And when he reached the house of Cornelius, he said this: "God, I now know, doesn't have any favorite nations, but welcomes every person who is willing to obey him."

He told Cornelius and his family all about Jesus. The spirit of God was on them. So Peter said they should be baptized.

Leviticus 11; Acts 10.

The Adventures of Paul

Once everyone had agreed that all nations could become Christian, there was nothing to stop Paul and his friends going everywhere to tell people about Jesus. And he did. He went to Syria, Turkey, Greece – all over the Bible lands. Often he would go back to a town where he had already spread the word of Jesus to see how his friends were getting on.

Wherever Paul was he would talk of Jesus. Sometimes just after getting off the boat he would see a group of people watching the bustle of boats coming and going. Paul would go over and preach Jesus' ideas.

Paul in Prison

Wherever Paul went, his enemies would try to get him into trouble. But he didn't care. He would talk to those who looked after him when he was in prison, and they would learn about Jesus.

Sometimes telling people about Jesus showed them that the gods they themselves worshiped were false. Once Paul and a friend called Silas were in the town of Philippi. A girl lived there who used to tell people's fortunes. She never told the truth, because she was in the grip of an evil spirit. But she was a slave, and her owners made a lot of money by getting people to pay her to tell their fortunes.

This girl started to follow Paul every day, shouting, "Here are the servants of the Most High God, they have come to tell you how to be saved." Eventually Paul lost his temper and said to the spirit, "I order you in the name of Jesus to leave that woman." And the spirit left her. She no longer told these

foolish fortunes. But her owners were very angry. They could no longer make any money out of her. So they got hold of Paul and Silas, and told those in charge of Philippi that the two Christians were doing evil things. Paul and Silas were beaten many times and thrown into prison.

That night, there was an earthquake. The prison shook and its doors flew open. Chains fell off the prisoners. The man who looked after them was going to kill himself, because he thought the prisoners had escaped. But Paul told him not to worry. All the prisoners were still there. The man then saw how good Paul was. He decided he wanted to become a Christian. He took Paul and Silas to his home. He fed them and washed the wounds on their backs, where they had been beaten. And all the people who lived in his house were baptized.

Acts 16, 16–34.

Paul in Greece

At another time Paul was in a Greek city called Ephesus. He was with two Christian friends called Gaius and Aristarchus. They were telling everyone that gods made by human hands were not gods at all.

This very much annoyed some men who made money from selling little silver models of a goddess called Diana. They believed that a huge statue of Diana had fallen from heaven long ago into the city of Ephesus. They also knew that if everyone realized that Diana was not a real god, no one would buy their statues.

So they got lots of people to make trouble on the streets. The great crowd caught Paul's friends Gaius and Aristarchus and pulled them into the theater. For two hours people shouted and screamed "Diana of Ephesus is great."

But in the end Gaius and Aristarchus got away safely.

But sometimes Paul knew that people who worshiped other gods were really trying to find the true God. When he was in Greece he walked up and down the city of Athens, admiring the beautiful buildings. He came across an altar, with the words, "To an unknown God" written on it. This pleased him, because everywhere else in that city were hundreds of false gods.

So he made a speech about this altar. He told those listening that God had made everyone in the world. "We are all children of God," said Paul. So, he said, it was silly to suppose we could be children of something made with our own hands, like these false gods in Athens. But he told them that their altar "To an unknown God" showed that they wanted to worship the God Paul knew really did exist, even though they didn't know him.

Then he told them about Jesus. When he came to the part where Jesus rose from the dead, many people laughed. They couldn't believe that. But a few wanted to hear more. And some men and women became Christians because of what Paul had told them.

Paul was very busy in Greece and he did not always have time to return to the towns he had already visited, so Paul used to write letters to these Christians giving them advice and encouragement.

Acts 17, 16–34.

Paul Goes to Rome

Most of all Paul wanted to go to Rome, where Caesar lived. This was at that time the greatest city in the world. The Romans ruled nearly everywhere.

Paul thought of a very clever way of getting to Rome. His enemies were always trying to put him on trial. Paul had the right to be tried for anything in Rome, if he wanted to. So every time an enemy tried to bring him to trial, Paul said, "I must be tried in Rome." In the end, he knew they would have to take him there.

Even so, it was not easy to reach Rome. To get there meant a dangerous sea voyage. Paul set sail, guarded by a Roman soldier. As they journeyed, the weather grew worse and worse. When they stopped at a harbor in Crete, Paul said it was too dangerous to go on. But nobody listened to him.

The skies grew dark. The northeast wind became stronger. The storms were terrible. For many days no one could see the sky or the sun or the stars. In the hope that the boat wouldn't sink, they threw overboard nearly all their goods, to make it lighter.

By now many of the sailors and passengers were certain they were going to drown. But Paul knew God intended him to reach Rome. He stood up in the boat and told everyone not to be afraid. He said that God's messenger had appeared to him, saying that since Paul had to reach Rome, all the other two-hundred and seventy-six people in the boats would too.

They had become so miserable and scared that for fourteen days none of them had eaten anything. Paul took some bread, thanked God for it, broke it and ate it. This gave everyone else more courage, so they all ate something.

But the dangers were not over. As day dawned, they could see an island with a beach ahead of them. They raised the sails. The boat headed for the beach. But the currents were too strong and it ran aground. The front part stuck fast and the back part began to break up. Everyone had to leap overboard and swim for the shore.

The island was called Malta. On the shore they lit a fire, to dry themselves. The people on the island looked after them. Two amazing things happened. First, a snake bit him as he was putting wood on the fire. Everybody thought he would die of poisoning, but he simply shook the snake off his arm and it fell into the fire. He was perfectly well.

He also amazed people because when the father of the man who was in charge of Malta fell ill, Paul made him better by saying prayers and putting his hands on him. After this, other sick people on the island came to Paul to be healed.

They waited three months in Malta, until it was safe to sail again. Another boat took them to Rome. There Paul waited for trial in his own rooms, looked after by a soldier.

So for two years Paul stayed in Rome awaiting trial. He wrote many letters from Rome about Christianity.

Acts 19, 23–41; Acts 25, 13–27; Acts 26–28.

The Best Gift of All

Paul asked himself what was the best gift any person could possess. Was it the gift of being able to speak well? Was it the gift of being able to understand everything? Was it the ability to do wonderful things which amazed other people? Was it the gift of being generous and giving away money to those who needed it?

Paul decided it was none of these gifts. These were all good. But greater than any of these was loving people.

What does it mean to love people? Loving people means being kind and patient. Love never shows off. Love isn't pleased when other people are wicked. But love forgives people. Those who love are never rude or selfish. And they

236

don't hate others.

"It is good to believe," said Paul. "It is good to show that God has prepared wonderful things for us. But best of all is to love people."

Then Paul thought of the famous story told in the writings of the prophet Samuel of how kind David was to Mephibosheth, the son of Jonathan whom David loved. Mephibosheth was crippled in both feet. David gave him all the goods of Saul, Jonathan's father, and made him eat at the king's table all the days of his life.

Love truly is the best gift of all.

II Samuel 9; I Corinthians 13.

237